IMAGES
of America

JEFFERSON CITY

IMAGES
of America

JEFFERSON CITY

Linda T. Gass and Albert L. Lang

ARCADIA
PUBLISHING

Published by Arcadia Publishing
Charleston, South Carolina

Library of Congress Control Number: 2014934090

For all general information, please contact Arcadia Publishing:
Telephone 843-853-2070
Fax 843-853-0044
E-mail sales@arcadiapublishing.com
For customer service and orders:
Toll-Free 1-888-313-2665

Visit us on the Internet at www.arcadiapublishing.com

To my parents, Howard and Martha Lang, and my brother
Peter for teaching me the precious value of home

—Albert L. Lang

I dedicate this book to my parents, Hollis and Mae Talley.
They taught me about my ancestors and the area in which
I lived, and helped me to find my "sense of place."

—Linda T. Gass

CONTENTS

Acknowledgments

This book has been a labor of love to honor those that have made Jefferson City the special place we call home. We are in debt to many who shared images and their stories. This is not a comprehensive history but instead a collection of available images fitting into the space allowed. Unless otherwise noted, images appear courtesy of the Mildred L. Iddins Special Collections, Carson-Newman University.

Special thanks to Helen Jolley and Alice Pryor for their wonderful images and gracious assistance. We are indebted to Cleve Smith for his extensive editing of chapter two and most of its images, along with the numerous historical documents, photographs, and facts he provided.

We are very grateful to Betty Catlett for all her help and for sharing so many of her family's treasured photographs. Thanks to Barbara Peck Dean and the Stephen Peck family for their photographs and history. We are grateful to John Fain for his images and assistance. Appreciation to Ronnie Housely for dropping off any photographs he thought we could use. Thanks to Nancy Dalton for invaluable images. We are thankful to the First United Methodist Church for several photographs. Our gratitude also goes to Juanita Franklin and Dennis Raper for many wonderful images. Thanks to Charles Key for his help and photographs and Libby Gardner for her assistance and images. We are grateful for the assistance of Paul and Imogene Brewer in whatever project we are working on.

We would also like to thank Ann Acuff, Appalachian Electric Cooperative, Janice Brown, Bernard Bull, Ginger Poe Burchett, Becky Burks, Mitch Cain, Bryon Caldwell, Jim Collins, Aileen Combs, Mark Dean, Barbara Dyer, Michael Evon, Nancy Farris, Janie Talley Gass, Patrick Gass, Dave Gentry, the *Grainger County News*, Helen Gray, Ernie Hedges, Lu Hinchey, Susie Blanc Jarnagin, the Jefferson City Mayor's Office, Jefferson County Archives, the *Jefferson Standard Banner*, the Los Angeles Angels of Anaheim, the *Morristown Citizen Tribune*, Mary Evelyn Musick, Barbara Parker, Beverly Phipps, the Pittsburgh Pirates, Opalee Queen, Roverta Russaw, Barron Smith, Helen Tarr, the Tennessee State Library and Archives, and Lisa Williams.

Thanks to our wonderful colleagues at Carson-Newman University's Stephens-Burnett Memorial Library for their encouragement. Special thanks to Lisa Flanary and Garrett Nunn.

Thanks to Charlie, whose memory is better than mine, and our four boys—Michael, Brian, Patrick, and Brent—who never seem to tire of hearing about my current project.

Thank you to my wife, Cindy, and my children—Harper, Maggie, and Gracie Li—who are constant reminders of how much God has blessed me.

INTRODUCTION

In 1972, David and Holly Franke listed Jefferson City in their book *Safe Places* as one of the safest places to live in America, stating that "crime was low, beauty abundant, and plenty of recreational areas exist for the whole family." One wonders how Adam and Elizabeth Peck would have reacted. Little did they realize they would be credited with being the first settlers of the community this was written about over 180 years later. Leaving Virginia, they traveled southward down the Holston River, arriving in 1788 on the banks of Mossy Creek. Named for its plentiful and distinctive moss growth, the area would become home. Finding the remains of a crudely built fort, they had temporary shelter until they could construct a log cabin. Utilizing the five-mile-long waterway's power, they built a gristmill that served an ever-growing area.

With the arrival of additional settlers, Elizabeth Peck asked Adam to build a place of worship. Completed in 1790, it was named Elizabeth's Chapel. One of the Pecks' slaves, "Uncle John," whom Elizabeth had taught to read, was selected to be the area's first regular preacher, serving black and white parishioners of various denominations.

The region continued to grow, and on June 11, 1792, Gov. William Blount signed the ordinance creating Jefferson and Knox Counties out of Greene and Hawkins Counties. A Revolutionary War veteran, Adam Peck became a member of the initial Tennessee Assembly, which drafted Tennessee's constitution in 1796. Peck also served as one of Jefferson County's justices of the peace, and was also one of Knoxville's founders.

Carson-Newman University had its beginnings on Mossy Creek's east bank in 1851, as Baptists sought to offer better-prepared ministers to local congregations. Founded as Mossy Creek Missionary Baptist Seminary, the school was named Carson College in 1880 and existed for several years alongside Newman College, a separate facility for the education of women. In 1889, the two colleges united as one of the first coeducational Baptist institutions. Over 160 years later, the university continues to prepare students academically and spiritually, steeped in the ideals of truth, beauty, and goodness.

In the early 1830s, zinc ore was discovered east of Mossy Creek, but it was not until 1854 that Benjamin Branner established what was considered the first operational mine. The East Tennessee Zinc Company took over control in 1867, and during the ensuing decades, three major mining companies worked mines in the area: the American Zinc Company of Tennessee, the Universal Exploration Company (a subsidiary of US Steel), and the New Jersey Zinc Company. At one time, the Jefferson City mine located off Highway 92 was the second-largest zinc producer in the nation.

In 1858, the East Tennessee & Virginia Railroad route from Bristol to Knoxville was completed, helping provide easier access to cities east and west. John Roper Branner gave the land for the right-of-way through Mossy Creek but insisted that all passenger trains would stop at the local station. Passengers would arrive via railroad until the mid-1950s.

Mossy Creek did not escape the Civil War. The Confederate army had controlled Knoxville from the time of Tennessee's secession from the Union on June 8, 1861. In September, Gen.

Ambrose Burnside liberated the city, but on November 17 Gen. James Longstreet laid siege to Knoxville in an attempt to reclaim it for the Confederacy. Defeated, Longstreet turned his army eastward. Several skirmishes ensued over the next month, including the Battle of Mossy Creek, on December 29, 1863. Although a moral victory for the Union, neither side advanced their position despite seven hours of fighting and over 500 casualties.

In the ensuing decades, two other communities sprang up around Mossy Creek. The Carsonville section, to the south, was named after Carson & Peak General Merchandise owner J.R.N. Carson. The Frame Addition community was to the west and was named after real estate investor and newspaperman Sam M. Frame. Although separated by farmland, these communities joined with Mossy Creek and were incorporated as Jefferson City in February 1901.

The Tennessee Valley Authority (TVA) began buying up land for the creation of a dam and Cherokee Lake during the late 1930s. Reluctantly, many people gave up their homes and farms for the promise of electricity and flood control. Construction brought many people to Jefferson City, and it continued to grow. Completed in 1940, the lake became a favorite recreational spot for locals and tourists.

In 1976, the city celebrated its diamond jubilee in conjunction with the nation's bicentennial. In 2001, the city celebrated its centennial, while Carson-Newman enjoyed its sesquicentennial. Over 225 years after Adam and Elizabeth Peck's arrival, the community they began is still growing and flourishing. Revitalization efforts are under way in the historic downtown area, as well as other civic improvements. The city's official website nicely sums up its current community outlook: "Civic pride in Jefferson City is reflected in the city's ongoing efforts to build a better future, while striving to retain meaningful connections to its past." The Pecks would be proud.

One

SETTLERS ON THE BANKS
FOUNDATIONS AND
HISTORICAL HAPPENINGS

Once providing the name for what is now Jefferson City, Mossy Creek is a five-mile-long waterway that winds its way northeastward to meet the Holston River. From the time of the area's earliest settlers, the creek provided a means of survival and growth. The Pecks used its waters for their gristmill in the 1780s, while Carson-Newman University had its beginnings on its east bank in 1851. Although it is reduced in size, its influence and heritage are still felt today.

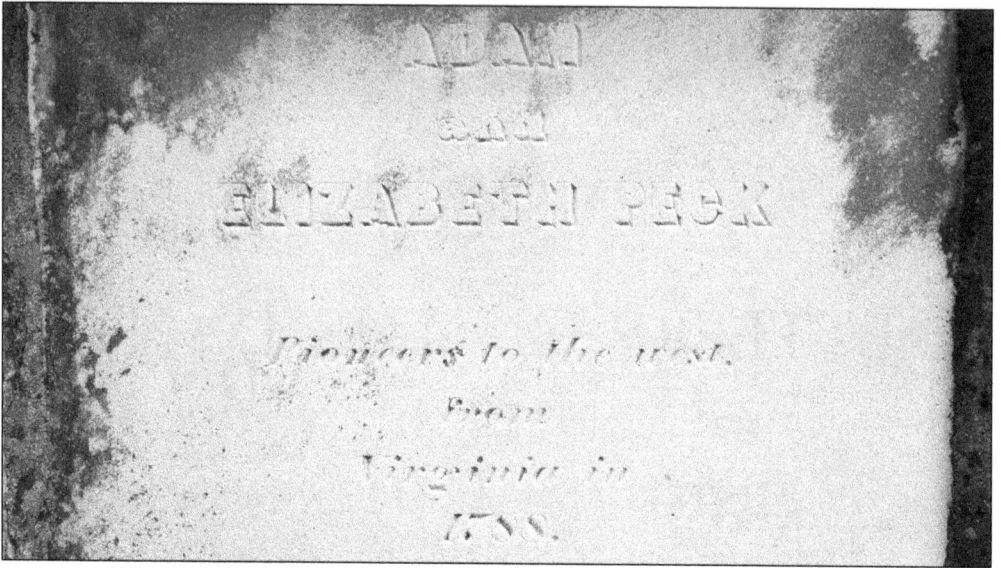

Adam and Elizabeth Peck are credited with being the first settlers in this area, traveling from Virginia along the Holston River and arriving in 1788. They occupied a crude fort for protection and then eventually built a log cabin on a site located near what is now Cherokee Drive. Utilizing the waterpower of Mossy Creek, the Pecks' gristmill thrived within what became a growing community. The gristmill was active until 1941. Adam became a member of the initial Tennessee Assembly, which drafted Tennessee's constitution, served as one of Jefferson County's justices of the peace, and was one of Knoxville's founders. The Pecks are buried in the Old Methodist Cemetery, now part of Westview Cemetery. (Photograph by Charles Key.)

Adam Peck was born near Sharpsburg in Frederick County, Maryland, in 1757. Before moving to Virginia, Peck served in the Maryland Line during the Revolutionary War, where he became an ensign on January 12, 1781, under Capt. P. Lockhart. This marker was placed by the Daughters of the American Revolution in 1956. (Photograph by Charles Key.)

Adam Peck purchased additional property and received land grants for his role in the Revolutionary War. The total area owned by the Pecks amounted to around five square miles, much of which is now under Cherokee Lake. Members of the Peck family operated a mill on the site for 146 years until TVA bought the land and ordered it torn down in 1941. Pictured are the mill's ruins in Mossy Creek. (Courtesy of Ernie Hedges.)

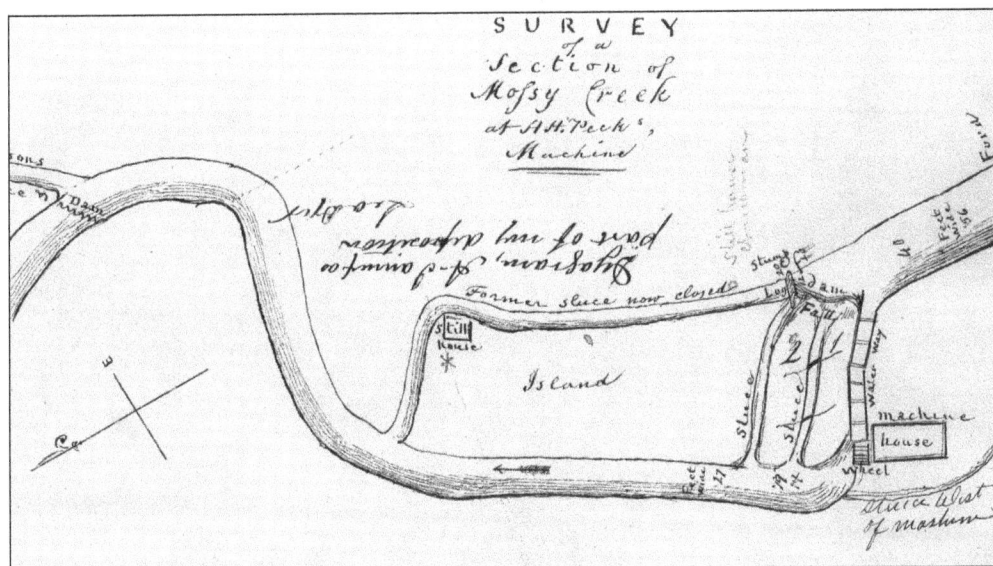

This early survey map was a diagram used as part of a legal deposition. It shows in detail the extent of Adam Peck's mill operation, referred to as his "machine." One of the original millstones was placed at Glenmore Mansion in 2008. (Courtesy of Jefferson County Archives.)

With the arrival of additional settlers who were mostly Methodist, Elizabeth Peck asked Adam to build a church where they could worship. The church was called Elizabeth's Chapel and was completed in 1790. Elizabeth had taught one of their slaves, known as "Uncle John," to read. He was selected to be the area's first regular preacher and served both black and white parishioners, as well as those of other denominations. (Photograph by Charles Key.)

In 1842, British immigrant J. Gray Smith published *A Brief Historical, Statistical and Descriptive Review of East Tennessee, United States of America Developing Its Immense Agricultural, Mining, and Manufacturing Advantages, with Remarks to Emigrants.* Smith included this lithograph in his book, highlighting the region's beauty, which was so attractive to the Pecks. (Courtesy of Map and Lithograph Collection, Special Collections, University of Tennessee, Knoxville—Libraries.)

12

Pres. George Washington appointed William Blount governor of the "Territory South of the River Ohio" in 1790. On June 11, 1792, Blount signed the ordinance creating Jefferson and Knox Counties out of Greene and Hawkins Counties. A proponent of statehood, Blount served as chairman for the Knoxville convention that drafted Tennessee's constitution in 1796 and then as one of its first senators. (Courtesy of Tennessee State Library and Archives.)

While only five miles long, Mossy Creek's power proved attractive to other entrepreneurs like Adam Peck. By 1836, an iron works, an ax handle factory, a wool-carding operation, and a cotton-spinning factory had all shared the creek's banks. William Cox purchased land in 1796 and added his gristmill to the growing community around 1803. It was later known as Mill Springs Mill and was in use until the 1950s. It is the county's only mill listed in the National Register of Historic Places.

Sometime around 1835, George Branner built a gristmill on Mossy Creek's west bank. Over 30 years later, it had fallen into disrepair, but it was revived by Frank Jarnigan, who did an extensive restoration, including adding a second story. Later known as the Jefferson City Milling Company, it was locally referred to as the Old Mossy Creek Mill. It was operational until 1951 and destroyed by arsonists in the mid-1960s.

A family dressed up for an outing stopped to have their picture taken on Mossy Creek, with the falls for a backdrop. (Courtesy of Helen Jolley.)

Mossy Creek Missionary Baptist Seminary (now Carson-Newman University) opened its doors for its first session in September 1851 in the Mossy Creek Baptist Church building. By decade's end, the school boasted an administration building and two dormitories. Enrollment was around 150 students, including 75 in the preparatory department. Four faculty taught all courses, and tuition ranged from $10 (preparatory) to $18 (senior).

This 1890s view of Mossy Creek shows the railroad, the R.M. Bales (later Moser) livery stable under construction, and the woolen mill in the background. (Courtesy of Nancy Dalton.)

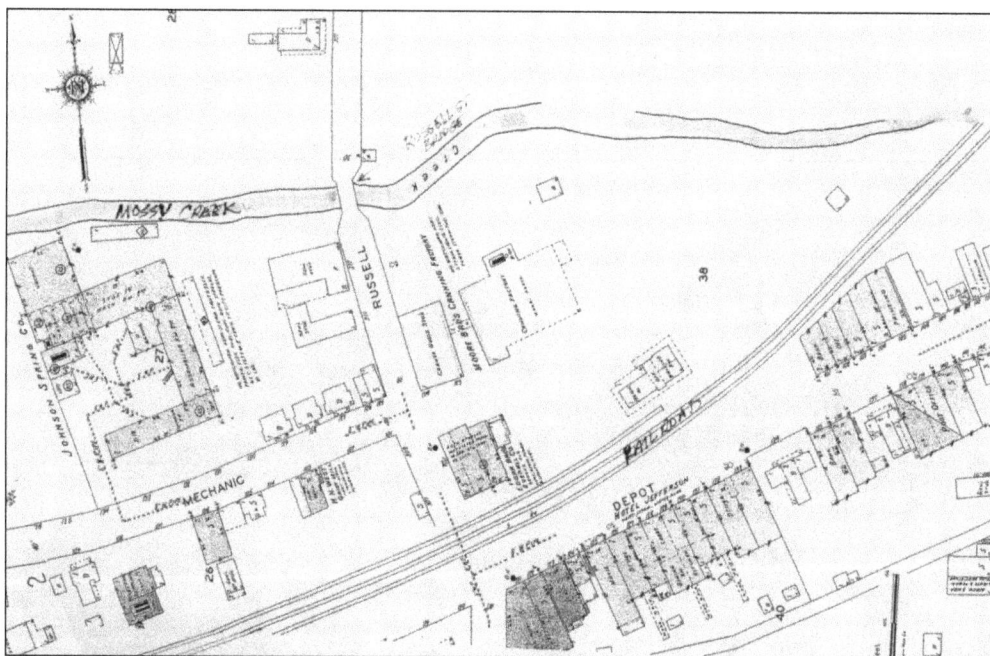

This 1929 map gives a glimpse of the businesses located on the north side of downtown. Included are the post office; the Mossy Creek Bank, in its last days; the First National Bank; the Hotel Jefferson, flanked by two drugstores; and the movie theater. They are all on Depot Street. On the other side of the railroad are the Moore Brothers Canning Factory and the Edgar Brothers Overall Company. Heading west were the H.H. Grist Mill, the Johnson Spring Company, and the Jefferson City Lumber Company.

In the early 1830s, iron ore was discovered east of Mossy Creek. In 1854, Benjamin Branner established what was considered the first operational mine. After the Civil War, the East Tennessee Zinc Company, which Mossy Creek's William Saltar Sizer helped organize, briefly took over control in 1867. During the ensuing decades, the three major mining companies working mines in the area were the American Zinc Company of Tennessee, the Universal Exploration Company (a subsidiary of US Steel), and the New Jersey Zinc Company. At one time, the Jefferson City mine off of Highway 92 was the second-largest zinc producer in the nation. (Courtesy of Betty Catlett.)

One of Mossy Creek's most influential citizens, John Roper Branner (1822–1869), began his career running a store with his brother in the basement of the family tavern in Dandridge. Moving to Mossy Creek, he continued in several business enterprises and real estate investments through which he increased his wealth. He also served as president of the East Tennessee, Virginia & Georgia Railroad. In 1868–1869, he built the home he christened The Oaks (later named Glenmore Mansion) but died before he could take up residence. (Courtesy of Tennessee State Library and Archives.)

Illustrating a constant and vital part of Jefferson City's history, this 1922 photograph shows a railroad crew building a culvert. (Courtesy of Tennessee State Library and Archives.)

In 1858, the East Tennessee & Virginia Railroad Company's route from Bristol to Knoxville was completed, providing easier access to cities on the East Coast and in the expanding West. John Roper Branner gave the land for the right-of-way through Mossy Creek with the provision that all passenger trains would stop at the local station. (Courtesy of Cleve Smith.)

The East Tennessee & Virginia Railroad and the East Tennessee & Georgia Railroad consolidated in 1869 to become the East Tennessee, Virginia & Georgia Railroad. It would go through another merger towards the end of the century, forming the Southern Railway. (Courtesy of Cleve Smith.)

From 1858 until the mid-1950s, trains brought commuters to Mossy Creek and, later, Jefferson City. This photograph is of the last passenger train, after which only freight trains came through town. (Courtesy of Betty Catlett.)

CHARTERS

of Jefferson City, Tennessee

Granted by the

State of Tennessee

CHAPTER 393.

Senate Bill No. 124.

An Act to incorporate the town of Mossy Creek, under the corporate name of Jefferson City, and to provide for the organization, powers, and government thereof, and to provide for the election of a Justice of the Peace of said city.

Section 1. Be it enacted by the General Assembly of the State of Tennessee, That the town of Mossy Creek, in Jefferson County, and the inhabitants thereof be and are hereby incorporated a body politic and corporate under and by the style and name of "Jefferson City", and shall have perpetual succession by this corporate name; may sue and be sued, grant, plead and be impleded, grant, receive, purchase, and hold real and personal property and dispose of the same for the benefit of the said city, and may have and use a city seal.

Boundaries.

Section 2. Be it further enacted, That the boundary and limits of said Jefferson City shall be as follows: Beginning in the center of the public road leading from Mrs. W. S. Sizer's across the hill toward the river at a point in said public road formerly known as the Tittsworth farm corner; thence due south in a right line to Sixth Avenue; in the Frame addition thence west with Sixth avenue and Seventh street; thence with said Seventh street to Ninth avenue and Davis line; thence with Ninth avenue and a direct line to the southeast corner of Hugh Cowan's property on the Mossy Creek and Dandridge road; thence east to the east side of the McCanless addition; thence north with said line to main road; thence west with said road to Welch's line and corner; thence in a northerly direction to the southwest corner of William Branner's farm; thence northerly with the Branner line to the northeast corner of the property now occupied by Mrs. Cochran; thence in a northerly direction a direct line to the northeast corner of J. F. Ross's yard; thence in a westerly direction, taking in Hugh L. William's residence to the beginning.

Prior to 1900, two other communities sprang up around Mossy Creek. Carsonville, named after J.R.N. Carson, owner of Carson & Peak General Merchandise and the nephew of James H. Carson, one of Carson-Newman's founders, was to the south. To the west was the Frame Addition community, named after real estate investor and newspaperman Sam M. Frame. Although separated by farmland, these communities joined with Mossy Creek and were incorporated as Jefferson City in February 1901. John T. Henderson, president of Carson-Newman, and Ralph Mountcastle were instrumental in changing the name. Businessmen thought "Mossy Creek" too quaint and were often called "Moss Backs" in their travels. Despite considerable opposition to a change, Jefferson City was chosen in honor of the former president and as an attempt to relocate the county seat.

Serving in 43 divisions, nearly 100,000 Tennesseans served in World War I, including over 550 from Jefferson County. Locally, under the leadership of school presidents Jesse McGarity Burnett and William Lee Gentry, Carson-Newman weathered the trying days of the war. Enrollment dropped as students left for military service, but thanks to the implementation of a Student Army Training Corps, the college remained afloat.

In the 1930s, a Civilian Conservation Corps (CCC) camp was located on the hill overlooking Jefferson City. The men worked on projects ranging from soil conservation to building fire towers, erecting phone lines, and constructing roads. The camp had its own motor pool, mess hall, and army-style barracks. Some of the men married local girls and remained in Jefferson City. (Courtesy of Bernard Bull.)

During World War II, Carson-Newman contracted with the Navy for a pre-officer training Navy V-12 unit. The program lasted from July 1, 1943, until June 30, 1945. During this period, several hundred Navy men trained while living on campus. They published a biweekly newsletter called *The Periscope* and had their own orchestra and choir. They also participated in intramurals and intercollegiate athletics. A three-semester academic year was set up, which reverted to a two-semester program with the termination of the program. (Courtesy of Barbara Dyer.)

During the late 1930s, the Tennessee Valley Authority (TVA) began buying up land to build a dam and create Cherokee Lake. Many people reluctantly gave up their homes and farms for the promise of electricity and flood control. The dam's construction brought many people to Jefferson City, businesses profited, and the town grew. The dam was completed in 1940, and the lake became a favorite recreational area offering opportunities for camping, picnicking, and swimming. (Courtesy of Janice Brown.)

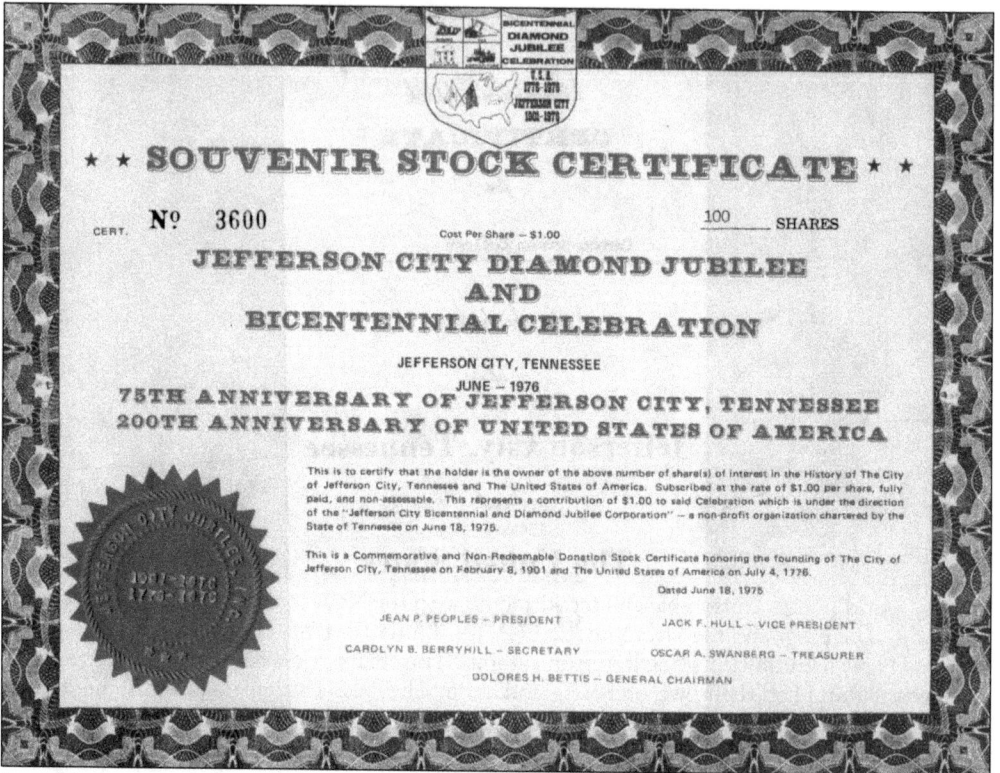

SOUVENIR STOCK CERTIFICATE

CERT. N0 3600

Cost Per Share — $1.00

100 SHARES

JEFFERSON CITY DIAMOND JUBILEE
AND
BICENTENNIAL CELEBRATION

JEFFERSON CITY, TENNESSEE

JUNE – 1976

75TH ANNIVERSARY OF JEFFERSON CITY, TENNESSEE
200TH ANNIVERSARY OF UNITED STATES OF AMERICA

This is to certify that the holder is the owner of the above number of share(s) of interest in the History of The City of Jefferson City, Tennessee and The United States of America. Subscribed at the rate of $1.00 per share, fully paid, and non-assessable. This represents a contribution of $1.00 to said Celebration which is under the direction of the "Jefferson City Bicentennial and Diamond Jubilee Corporation" — a non-profit organization chartered by the State of Tennessee on June 18, 1975.

This is a Commemorative and Non-Redeemable Donation Stock Certificate honoring the founding of The City of Jefferson City, Tennessee on February 8, 1901 and The United States of America on July 4, 1776.

Dated June 18, 1975

JEAN P. PEOPLES – PRESIDENT   JACK F. HULL – VICE PRESIDENT

CAROLYN B. BERRYHILL – SECRETARY   OSCAR A. SWANBERG – TREASURER

DOLORES H. BETTIS – GENERAL CHAIRMAN

In 1976, the city celebrated its diamond jubilee along with the nation's bicentennial. Historical booklets were produced and pageants were held, along with parades, fashion shows, and sporting events to commemorate the milestones.

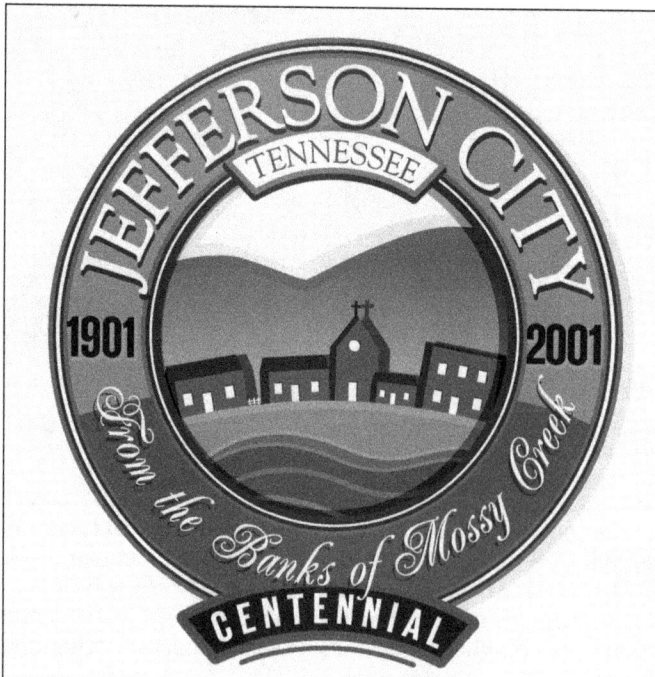

In 2001, the city organized a birthday party to celebrate its centennial. Events included a cake, a five-kilometer run/walk, a historical photograph exhibit, parades, and a special Old Time Saturday, which is held each October. In cooperation with Carson-Newman, the city created a city park and walking area that was christened Centennial Park. (Courtesy of Michael Evon.)

Two

THE BATTLE OF MOSSY CREEK

CIVIL WAR YEARS

From the time Tennessee seceded from the Union on June 8, 1861, Knoxville was under Confederate control. In September of that year, Gen. Ambrose Burnside liberated the city. On November 17, Gen. James Longstreet laid siege to Knoxville in an attempt to reclaim the pivotal city for the Confederacy. Defeated, Longstreet turned his army eastward. Several skirmishes ensued over the next month, including the Battle of Mossy Creek on December 29, 1863. While it was a moral victory for the Union, after seven hours of fighting and over 500 casualties, neither side advanced their position. (Photograph by Charles Key.)

One of the Confederacy's leading generals, Gen. James Longstreet, was known as Robert E. Lee's "Old War Horse." In late 1863, he was ordered to drive Burnside out of Knoxville and retake the city. After being defeated, he retreated to Russellville, where he set up a 25-mile defense line from Rutledge to Dandridge. Several skirmishes took place, leading up to the devastating battle on December 29, 1863, at Mossy Creek. In April 1864, Longstreet finally left East Tennessee and returned to the Army of Northern Virginia. (Courtesy of Cleve Smith, *Campaign to Nowhere*.)

After Gen. Ambrose Burnside's resignation, Maj. Gen. John G. Foster took over control of the region's Federal army in Knoxville. Moving east, he found Longstreet prepared to force an engagement. Injured when his horse fell, Foster was forced to stay in Knoxville. He sent Brig. Gen. Samuel D. Sturgis of the Department of the Ohio with a large force of cavalry and some infantry across the Holston River into Jefferson County to drive Longstreet from East Tennessee, resulting in the local battles that caused much devastation to the valley. (Courtesy of Cleve Smith, *Campaign to Nowhere*.)

A career military man, Brig. Gen. Samuel D. Sturgis was born on June 11, 1822, in Shippensburg, Pennsylvania. After pursuing Longstreet from Strawberry Plains, Sturgis took Mossy Creek and advanced toward Talbott. Trying to outmaneuver the enemy and having sent part of his forces to Dandridge on December 29, Sturgis put his army at a disadvantage. Despite a driving surge by the Confederates, the Federal army withstood the barrage and with reinforcements remained in control of the town. (Courtesy of Cleve Smith, *Campaign to Nowhere*.)

With Confederate forces pressing the attack and Brig. Gen. Frank Armstrong overwhelming the Union's left flank, Col. James P. Brownlow felt that a sabre charge may be their only hope. Capt. E.J. Cannon led the 1st Tennessee Calvary, and though he and his horse were shot simultaneously, Brownlow's men were able to stop the advance for the first time that day. (Courtesy of Cleve Smith, *Campaign to Nowhere*.)

Capt. Eli Lilly was born on July 8, 1838, in Maryland. His family moved to Indiana, where he studied pharmacology and opened a drugstore in 1860. The next year, he joined the Union ranks, serving as captain of the 18th Battery, Indiana Light Artillery. The winter of 1863 saw Lilly and his men involved in expelling the Confederate army from East Tennessee. During the battle of Mossy Creek, Lilly's heroic leadership helped preserve a Union victory when his artillery unleashed over 500 rounds in three hours. After the war, he opened Eli Lilly & Company, one of the country's foremost pharmaceutical manufacturers. (Courtesy of Cleve Smith, *Campaign to Nowhere.*)

This map depicts the site of the day's fiercest fighting. As Southern forces rapidly approached, forming a horseshoe around the Union troops, the stage was set for a Confederate victory; however, with the growing loss of men and ammunition along with approaching Union reinforcements, they were forced to retreat. It was here that Capt. Eli Lilly made his heroic artillery stand in the center of the conflict. (Courtesy of Cleve Smith, *Campaign to Nowhere.*)

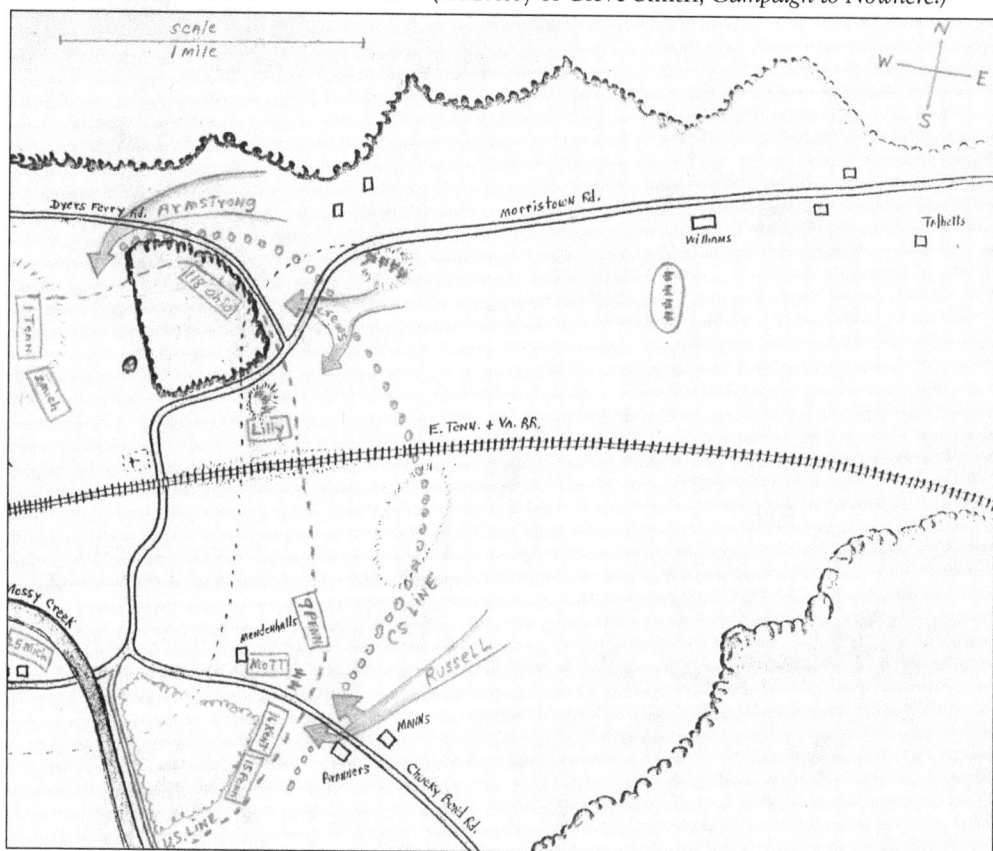

One of the more moving stories to come from the Battle of Mossy Creek involved Capt. Elbert J. Cannon. He and his horse were shot down while leading the 1st East Tennessee Cavalry against Brig. Gen. Frank Armstrong's Confederate forces. Hearing his call for help, the two Confederates who had fired on Cannon came to his side and, at his request, contacted his family in Talbott Station, where the Confederate States Army (CSA) was encamped. Cannon's mother was brought to her son's side and stayed with him until he died three days later. (Courtesy of Cleve Smith, *Campaign to Nowhere*.)

Capt. Elbert J. Cannon's gravesite is located in the Branner Cemetery, west of the Tennessee National Guard Armory in Jefferson City. There is an error on the headstone, as the death date should read January 1, 1864. (Courtesy of Cleve Smith, *Campaign to Nowhere*.)

While personally opposed to secession, Maj. Gen. W.T. Martin entered the CSA and eventually rose to the rank of brigadier general. Serving under Longstreet in the East Tennessee campaign, Martin was above all cavalry troops and the commanding CSA general during the Battle of Mossy Creek; however, due to the Federals' valiant stand and with reinforcements on the way, Martin was forced to retreat. After the war, he served as a senator in the Mississippi State Legislature. (Courtesy of Cleve Smith, *Campaign to Nowhere*.)

Brig. Gen. Frank C. Armstrong was born on November 22, 1835, on the Choctaw Agency, Indian Territory, in Oklahoma and initially served in the Union army. Resigning his captain's commission, he then joined the CSA. By 1863, he was promoted and was in command of a cavalry division under Maj. Gen. W.T. Martin. During the Battle of Mossy Creek, Armstrong was able to advance his men deep into Federal territory, but that effort was checked by the sabre-led charge of Capt. E.J. Cannon. (Courtesy of Cleve Smith, *Campaign to Nowhere*.)

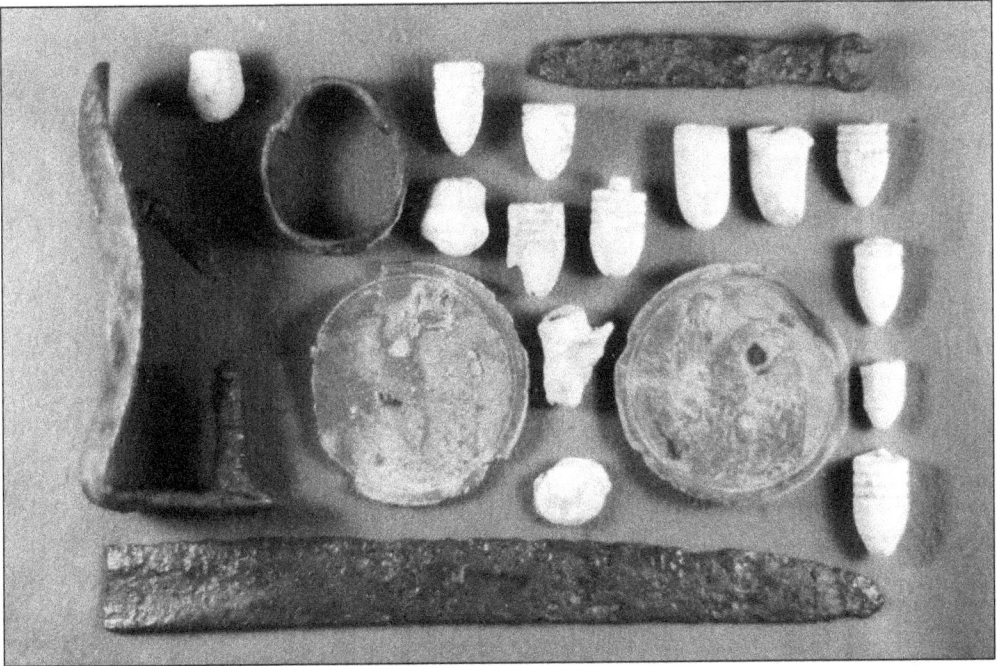

Over a 30-year period, Jefferson County resident Cleve Smith unearthed thousands of Civil War artifacts. Shown here is a sampling of relics, including buttons, various bullet types, and other items found in the woods left from the Battle of Mossy Creek. It was here that Brig. Gen. Frank C. Armstrong (CSA) pressured the forces of the 1st Tennessee Cavalry, 2nd Michigan Cavalry, and 118th Ohio Infantry to the north of the East Tennessee & Virginia Railroad and Morristown Road, but his advance was eventually repelled. (Both courtesy of Cleve Smith, *Campaign to Nowhere*.)

After Longstreet's retreat from Knoxville, Union forces pursued him eastward in an attempt to drive his forces from East Tennessee. Finding a strategic encampment near Morristown, he prepared to fight. In late December 1863, Union brigadier general Samuel D. Sturgis prepared for engagement as he moved his troops from New Market toward Dandridge and Mossy Creek. He utilized the site seen here as an encampment, where a small Methodist church founded by Elizabeth Peck once stood. (Courtesy of Cleve Smith, *Campaign to Nowhere*.)

Three

PILLARS OF THE COMMUNITY
NOTABLE CITIZENS

Mossy Creek/Jefferson City had many prominent citizens whose contributions space does not allow to detail. A few of its earlier residents listed in an 1873 gazetteer included carpenter, blacksmith, and railroad man J.M. Ashmore; merchant and builder J.C. Beeler; brothers Will and Oscar Godwin, who sold "fancy and staple groceries" along with confections, buggies, and harnesses; real estate agent A.J. Mountcastle; and Judge Milton Preston Jarnigan, who served as president of Mossy Creek Bank and Mossy Creek Woolen Mill and was a trustee of the University of Tennessee. (Courtesy of Helen Jolley.)

Col. Sam N. Fain operated a cotton-thread mill at Mossy Creek, where he built a home on the hill beside the mill. In 1862, Fain suffered financially when a shipment of his cotton was lost to fire on the Tennessee River during the Civil War near Huntsville. Although Fain was a staunch Southern supporter, he did not serve in the Confederacy. He was a charter member of the Presbyterian church. (Courtesy of John Fain.)

William Saltar Sizer was a partner and superintendent of the Wadsworth Sizer Paint Company in New Jersey. He came to Mossy Creek from New Jersey in 1866 when some New York investors sent him to pursue mining opportunities. He helped organize the East Tennessee Zinc Mine Company, whose ore was used in the production of paint and other products; however, after the backers ran out of money, the business failed. Sizer returned to the paint business and other local interests he had developed. He completed building his home, Seven Gables, in 1867. Sizer died on a business trip to Toledo, Ohio, in 1892. (Courtesy of Helen Jolley.)

John Richard Moser was born on February 25, 1867, and raised in Mossy Creek. The family home that once belonged to his grandfather Richard Hayworth was in the Black Oak area, long since covered by Cherokee Lake. He went to school in a one-room schoolhouse by a creek where students kept their buttermilk jars cold for lunch. He later attended Carson-Newman. Moser owned a livery stable for a time in the early 1900s and was one of the best-known sportsmen in the area, hunting a variety of animals, including panthers. He died on May 14, 1941. (Courtesy of Alice Pryor.)

George Timmons was born in 1848 and died in 1928, farming for most of his life. He was married to Mattie Martha Welby Rhoten. They had four daughters: Mattie, Helen, Emma, and Forrest. Emma Married Neil Brown Mims, and they had two sons, Hugh and George. George is remembered as a milk deliveryman for the city and a basketball coach at the local schools. Forrest Timmons wrote a society column for the newspaper for many years. (Courtesy of First United Methodist Church, Jefferson City.)

A graduate of Mossy Creek Baptist College, William Thomas Russell returned to teach mathematics and mechanical philosophy. In August 1882, he became the first and only president of Newman College and taught metaphysics as well as pure and applied mathematics. After the union with Carson College in 1889, he served as vice president, professor, and trustee for the coeducational institution. Russell was the first mayor of the newly incorporated Jefferson City (formerly Mossy Creek) from 1902 to 1903. (Photograph by Knaffe and Brakebill.)

Both graduates of Carson-Newman, the Butlers served the school throughout their lifetimes, giving of their time and money. D.L. Butler was a merchant and benefactor whose business career extended almost 50 years, including a mercantile store and numerous real estate holdings. He served 42 years on the board of trustees, 41 years on the executive committee, and was president of the alumni association as well as vice president of First National Bank. Bertie Maples Butler taught piano for a time in the music department. (Photograph by Tallent Photography.)

J.D. Bible was treasurer of Carson-Newman from 1915 to 1920 and also served as a trustee. During this time, he helped see the school through the tragic fire of 1916 in which the main administration building was completely destroyed. He also served as treasurer and on several committees at First Baptist Church. At the time of his death, on November 21, 1942, Bible had served as a Baptist deacon for 64 years. (Courtesy of Cleve Smith.)

Dana X. Bible was the son of J.D. Bible. He was born and raised in Jefferson City and attended Carson-Newman College, graduating in 1912. He was awarded an honorary doctorate in 1951. During his 34 years of coaching football, his teams won 14 major conference championships, including five at Texas A&M (where he started the "12th Man" tradition), six at Nebraska, and three at Texas. He also led Texas to the 1941 national championship, retiring in 1946 and serving as athletic director until 1956, with emeritus rank until his death in 1980. Bible finished with a 198-72-23 record and authored the popular *Championship Football* in 1947. He was elected into the College Football Hall of Fame in 1951. (Photograph by University Studio.)

Dr. Buford M. Tittsworth was born in Jefferson County in 1871. He was educated at Carson-Newman College and the University of Tennessee and was a graduate of Baltimore Medical College. (Courtesy of First United Methodist Church, Jefferson City.)

Long before the days of copays, this 1918 receipt shows Sam Rankin's charges of $1 for March's services paid in full. Dr. Tittsworth served the community with flexible morning and evening hours. (Courtesy of Cleve Smith.)

Dr. H.L. Tarr was born in 1881. He practiced medicine in Jefferson City until shortly before his death in 1952. His office was on Main Street, upstairs above Jefferson Hardware. At the time of his death, the *Jefferson County Standard* paid tribute to him by writing, "The night was never too dark, or the way too stormy, the path too difficult, for this plain and unassuming man to go out on an errand of help and mercy. He loved his profession. In the highest and best sense of the word, he was a true physician." (Courtesy of Helen Tarr.)

R.M. McCown was born in Sevier County in 1881. He began his medical practice in Sevierville, moved to Knoxville, and eventually settled in Jefferson City. Although he practiced general medicine, surgery was his specialty. In 1909, he married Nelle Blanche Tittsworth. He built the hospital on Jefferson Street and the doctors' offices beside it. He was elected mayor of Jefferson City in 1927. For years, he voluntarily offered his services to the Carson-Newman football team. The R.M. McCown Athletic Field was officially named for him in 1958. Dr. McCown died on April 14, 1961. (Courtesy of Jefferson City Mayor's Office.)

Dr. Frank L. Milligan was born in 1903 in Jefferson County. He and a friend opened a garage in Talbott, but he soon enrolled in medical school at Memphis. There, he met Mildred Osborne, whom he married in 1935. Milligan graduated in 1931 and did a two-year surgery residency at Baptist Hospital. He came back to Jefferson City, partnering with Dr. R.M. McCown. He enlisted in the Army after Pearl Harbor and was assigned to the Camp McCain Hospital in Mississippi but was soon sent to the Mayo Clinic for five months of surgical training. He was then transferred to Fort Jackson Hospital, near Columbia, South Carolina, where he became chief of surgery. He was discharged from the service in 1946, returned to Jefferson City, and began building a 15-bed clinic that operated until 1969. Dr. Milligan retired in 1984 and passed away on September 11, 1995.

Dr. Samuel Clark Fain was born in 1902 and attended medical school in Memphis. He served with Drs. McCown and Milligan at the Jefferson Hospital on Jefferson Street. At the end of World War II, Dr. Milligan practiced at his home until his clinic was finished. Dr. McCown eventually closed the hospital, but within a year Margaret Justice reopened the Jefferson Hospital in a smaller stone house on Russell Street. Dr. Fain took his patients there until the new facility opened in 1960. He practiced medicine until 1979 and passed away in 1981. Other local physicians of note were Drs. T.A. Caldwell, Earl Beets, E.P. Muncy, Eugene Howard, and John Ellis. (Courtesy of John Fain.)

Buford Bible was a graduate of the Carson-Newman class of 1927. He started teaching and coaching basketball that same year, retiring in 1968. He then taught at the University of Tennessee for 10 years after his retirement. Pictured from left to right are Bill Tarr, Lonas Tarr, Bible, and an unidentified Chevrolet representative.

Earl Rugel was born in 1916 and passed away in 1983. He followed in his father's footsteps as a wood craftsman. From an old wood plank building to a modern plant, the Rugels have been manufacturing church furniture since 1929. Earl's son Keith continues the business today. His daughter is Betty Catlett. (Courtesy of Betty Catlett.)

William Edward "Bill" Tate and Louis and Howard Ingram operated barbershops in several locations on Main Street. Tate was born in 1906 in Knoxville, and his family moved to Jefferson City when he was in his teens. He attended North Carolina A&T in Greensboro, North Carolina. He became a teacher and principal at the Riverview School in Dandridge. Tate taught recruits reading and writing skills during World War II. When he returned to Jefferson City, he began teaching school and helping out at Louis and Howard Ingram's barbershop. He bought into the business and remained there from 1945 until the 1970s. Many young men got their first haircuts from Bill Tate. (Courtesy of Barbara Peck Dean.)

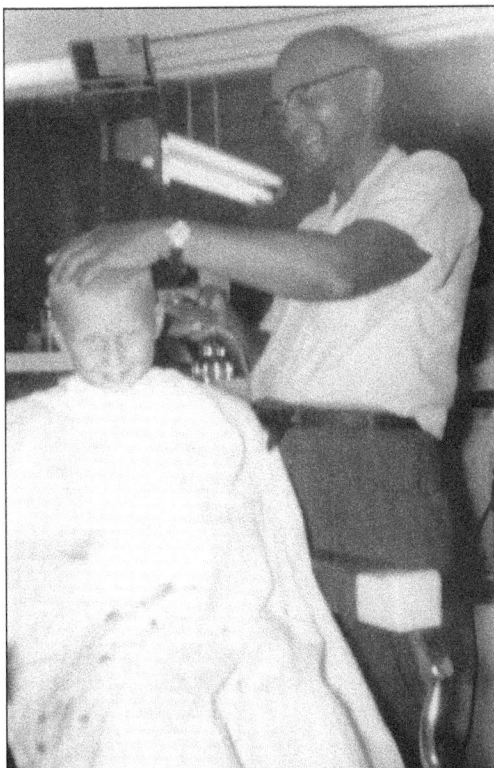

Madison Miller was born in 1924. He was a kind, gentle man who befriended many in the community. He and his brother C.V. and sister Shirley lived with their mother, Mrs. C.V. Miller, who operated a store on Main Street. Madison died in 1989. (Courtesy of Juanita Franklin.)

43

Evelyn "Mama Bird" Bryan Johnson was born in 1909. She earned her pilot's license in 1945 and by 1947 was a flight instructor. She was airport terminal executive and manager of Moore Murrell Airport in Morristown, beginning in 1953. She won many awards for her flying, including flight instructor of the year in 1973 and 1979, as well as inductions into the Women of Aviation Hall of Fame, the Tennessee Aviation Hall of Fame, and the National Aviation Hall of Fame. She entered the Guinness Book of World Records for the most flying time by a female pilot. She trained more than 5,000 pilots and gave FAA pilot exams to more than 9,000 hopefuls. She died in 2012 at the age of 102. (Courtesy of *Morristown Citizen-Tribune*.)

Dana Lauderback worked at the train depot for more than 50 years. He received the many packages from the trains, loaded them on a large flatbed wagon, and pulled it over to the depot, where he checked everything in and made sure they were delivered to the correct stores or individuals. Depending on the number of packages, he sometimes allowed children to climb on the wagon and ride to the depot. Lauderback died in 1976. (Diamond Jubilee Bicentennial Celebration.)

George Peck (left) started a dry-cleaning business on East Main Street in 1922. He was married to Willie Brown Moore, and together they raised a large family. He died in 1985. Also in the photograph is Howard Ingram, who was in the Navy during World War II, worked for the New Jersey Zinc Company, and learned to barber from his father, James Louis Ingram. He was married to Edith Ely, a schoolteacher, and they had one daughter, Dynese. Both served faithfully at Boyd Chapel United Methodist Church. (Courtesy of Roverta Russaw.)

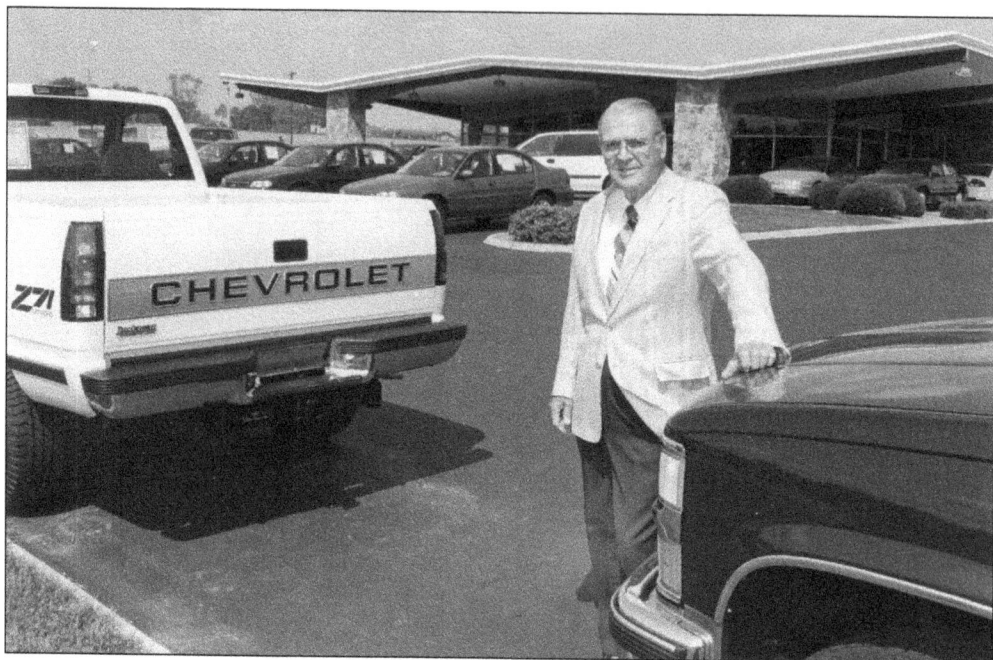

Lonas Tarr was born in 1920. A 1941 Carson-Newman graduate, he served in the US Army Air Corps during World War II as a pilot. After the war, he flew for American Airlines. He returned to Jefferson City when his father died in 1952. He purchased a Chevrolet dealership that year and was honored as a 50-year dealer in 2002. A trustee and benefactor of Carson-Newman and First Baptist Church, Tarr passed away in 2009.

Henry Blanc (left) was born in Jefferson City in 1928. He played football while at the College of William and Mary and was inducted into its athletic hall of fame. He was a member of First Baptist Church, served on the board of trustees of Carson-Newman, and was awarded an honorary doctorate degree in 1997. He joined Blanc & West Lumber Company in 1950, working until just shortly before his death in 1998. Adrian Blanc Jr. (right) was born in 1929. He was a graduate of Carson-Newman. He began working in the family business in 1951 and was on his way to work in 2001 when he suffered a heart attack and died. Both were known for their sense of humor, compassion, and loyalty. (Courtesy of Nancy Dalton.)

A direct descendant of "Uncle John" Peck, one of Adam and Elizabeth Peck's slaves, Eugene Peck graduated from Nelson Merry High School and attended Morristown College for one year. He stopped going to school to teach in a one-room school in Rocktown with 15 students. He later went back to school and graduated from Tennessee State College in 1950. He returned to Jefferson City and was principal of Nelson Merry School until Jefferson County schools were integrated. He then taught at Jefferson County High School, retiring after more than 45 years as principal and teacher. Peck died on March 2, 2003, at age 94. Ophelia Lowe Peck was a dental assistant for Drs. H.E. Hinton and W.P. Clear for more than 40 years. She died on November 22, 1998, at age 84. Their children are Stephen, Joseph "Michael," and Barbara. (Courtesy of Barbara Peck Dean.)

Pictured from left to right are Michael Peck, his wife Rachel, Stephen C. Peck, his wife Arlene, James O'Brien, Carolyn Peck, Stephen C. Peck II, and his wife Seana. Michael is a strategic account manager for Ventana Medical Systems, Inc. Stephen is a retired program analyst for TVA, and Arlene is a retired educator. James, Carolyn's husband, served on the police force in Detroit and is currently part of the University of Florida police force. Carolyn is a basketball analyst for ESPN. Stephen Jr. is a national evaluator at Peach State Hoops and the owner of Dreams in Motion Athletics. (Courtesy of the Peck family.)

Carolyn Peck is a graduate of Vanderbilt University. In 1999, she was named the Associated Press's Women's Basketball Coach of the Year, and she also became the first woman and African American to win the New York Athletic Club's Winged Foot Award after leading the Purdue Lady Boilermakers to their first national championship. She has also received the US Basketball Writers Association Coach of the Year, the WBCA Coach of the Year, and the Naismith College Coach of the Year awards. She was head coach and general manager of the WNBA's Orlando Miracle and head coach at the University of Florida. Peck was inducted into the Greater Knoxville Sports Writers' Hall of Fame, Vanderbilt's Hall of Fame, and the Tennessee Sports Hall of Fame. (Courtesy of the Peck family.)

Seated are James E. Dean and his wife, Barbara Peck Dean. Standing are Ophelia Dean, Mark Dean, and Mark's wife, Denise Jackson. James is a retired assistant superintendent of the TVA Cherokee Dams, including both Douglas and Norris Dams. Barbara worked for the Tennessee Department of Human Services in the bookkeeping department in the old First National Bank in Jefferson City. Ophelia is employed with TW Telecom as a field services specialist in the San Francisco Bay area. Mark and Denise recently returned to Tennessee after many years with IBM. (Courtesy of Barbara Peck Dean.)

Mark Dean is a graduate of the University of Tennessee and Florida Atlantic University and also holds a PhD in electrical engineering from Stanford University. He has developed a variety of computer systems and holds three of the nine patents for the original IBM personal computer. The invention of the Industry Standard Architecture (ISA) "bus," which permitted add-on devices like keyboards, disk drives, and printers to be connected to a motherboard, earned him and his colleagues' induction into the National Inventors Hall of Fame. He is currently the John Fisher Distinguished Professor at the University of Tennessee College of Engineering. (Courtesy of Mark Dean.)

Clyde Wright was born on February 20, 1943, in Jefferson City, where he played youth baseball. He graduated from Jefferson High School in 1961 and Carson-Newman in 1965, where he won the NAIA national baseball championship his senior year. He was drafted by the Los Angeles Angels and played eight years for the team. He pitched the first no-hitter ever thrown at Anaheim Stadium and won over 100 major-league games. He spent one year with Milwaukee and another with Texas and later played three years in Japan. (Courtesy of Angels Baseball.)

Phil Garner was born in Jefferson City in 1949. Drafted in the first round by the Oakland Athletics, Garner also played second and third base for the Pittsburgh Pirates, Houston Astros, Los Angeles Dodgers, and San Francisco Giants. He won the World Series with the Pirates in 1979. After his retirement in 1988, he was the manager for the Milwaukee Brewers, Detroit Tigers, and the Astros between 1992 and 2007. He was one of only 22 players in major-league history to hit a grand slam in consecutive games. (Courtesy of Pittsburgh Pirates.)

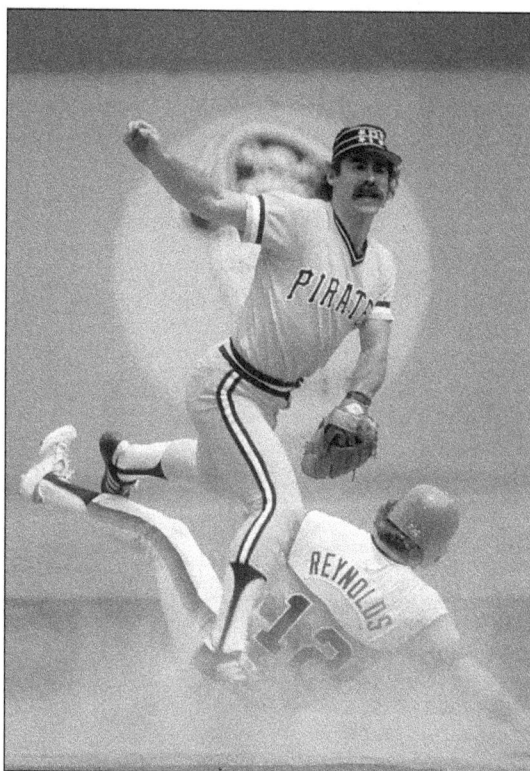

First team All-American linebackers, the Collins brothers both played at Jefferson County High School, transferred to Carson-Newman where they won an NAIA national championship, and were then drafted by NFL teams. Brent was chosen by the Buffalo Bills in 1990 and retired due to injury in 1992 after stops in Cincinnati and Miami. Todd was chosen by the New England Patriots in 1992. After seven years with the Patriots and one Super Bowl appearance, he signed with the St. Louis Rams in 1999, with whom he won Super Bowl XXXIV. He retired in 2001. (Courtesy of Jim Collins.)

Bryon Caldwell is currently a senior 3D animator for Framestore Visual Effects and Animation Studio in Montreal, Canada. He has worked for various studios, including Telltale Games, Disney's ImageMovers Digital, Sony Pictures Imageworks, and Dr. D Studios. Caldwell has worked on feature films such as *A Christmas Carol*, *Green Lantern*, *Happy Feet 2*, and *47 Ronin*. In 2014, his team won seven Oscars for their work on *Gravity*, as well as the British Academy of Film and Television Arts Award. Caldwell earned his master's degree in animation and visual effects from the Academy of Art University in San Francisco. He is a graduate of the digital media and design graphics program at East Tennessee State University and studied graphic design at Carson-Newman. (Courtesy of Bryon Caldwell.)

This 1940s Civitan Club picnic photograph shows, from left to right, (first row) Bill Catlett, Bud Hassell, Carl Skeen, Bill Swann, Morgan Johnson, Jim Whitaker, and Pat Holt; (second row) Cyril Dannenhold, Arnold Brokaw, unidentified, W.A. Bowen, John Murphy, "Hump" Havely, Chester Franklin, and Johnny O. Farris. (Courtesy of Betty Catlett.)

Pictured here in the 1980s are, from left to right, Dr. John Ellis, businessmen Henry Blanc, Adrian Blanc, and Buddy Catlett. Their collective contributions to the community spanned several decades. (Courtesy of Betty Catlett.)

Four

MEMORY LANES

STREET SCENES

Sometime during the 1950s, a Mr. Dickey waits outside the second railroad depot to catch a train home to Alabama after visiting family during the Christmas holidays. Not too long after, passenger trains were discontinued through Jefferson City. In the background are the businesses of East Main Street. (Courtesy of Barron Smith.)

This is an early photograph from around the turn of the 20th century facing east on the unpaved Depot Street (later Main Street). On the left is the mail arm utilized by trains and what was an orange fence allowing people to safely watch arriving and passing trains. On the right is Minnis & Zirkle, and a little farther down are the post office and the Yoe Hotel. (Diamond Jubilee Bicentennial Celebration.)

In another view of Main Street facing east, Draper & Darwin's dry goods store can be seen on the right, along with one of the downtown cafés. The Jefferson Theater was showing *The Mighty McGurk*, released in 1947 and starring Wallace Beery. Also seen are Hickey's Café and the Jefferson City Pharmacy. (Courtesy of Betty Catlett.)

In this 1940s photograph, Frances Bowman and "Brownie" Myers pose in front of Jefferson City Hardware. Behind them are the signs for Dr. H.L. Tarr and insurance agent H.H. Tittsworth. (Courtesy of Juanita Franklin.)

Looking west on Main Street, the Jefferson City Pharmacy, Butler Brothers clothing store, a barbershop, Skeen Furniture Company, and Hickey's Café are seen on the left. The Jefferson Theater showed another 1947 release, *The Guilt of Janet Ames*, starring Rosalind Russell, Melvyn Douglas, and Sid Caesar. Note the identifying Jefferson County "44" license plates. (Courtesy of Juanita Franklin.)

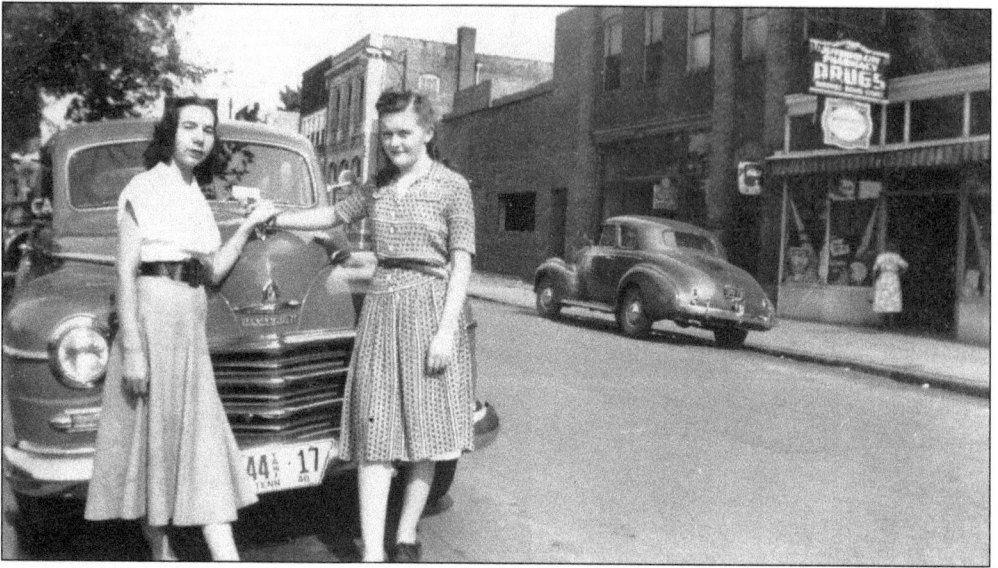

In the 1940s, Maxine Roberts (left) and Frances Bowman pose on Main Street with a Plymouth taxicab. Bowman worked for the Jefferson City Pharmacy for many years. (Courtesy of Juanita Franklin.)

Main Street in the late 1940s had a variety of businesses, including the Melody Theater, owned by Kendrick Hutton, as well as First National Bank, Lloyd May Clothing Company, and the J.B. Dick 5¢ & 10¢ store. (Courtesy of Juanita Franklin.)

Looking west again on Main Street, Skeen Furniture Company, Hickey's Café, the Jefferson Theater, and another café can be seen in the early 1940s. (Courtesy of Juanita Franklin.)

A 1955 Chevrolet station wagon waits on its owners as they run errands in Jefferson City Hardware and the Jefferson City Pharmacy down on Main Street. (Courtesy of Dennis Raper.)

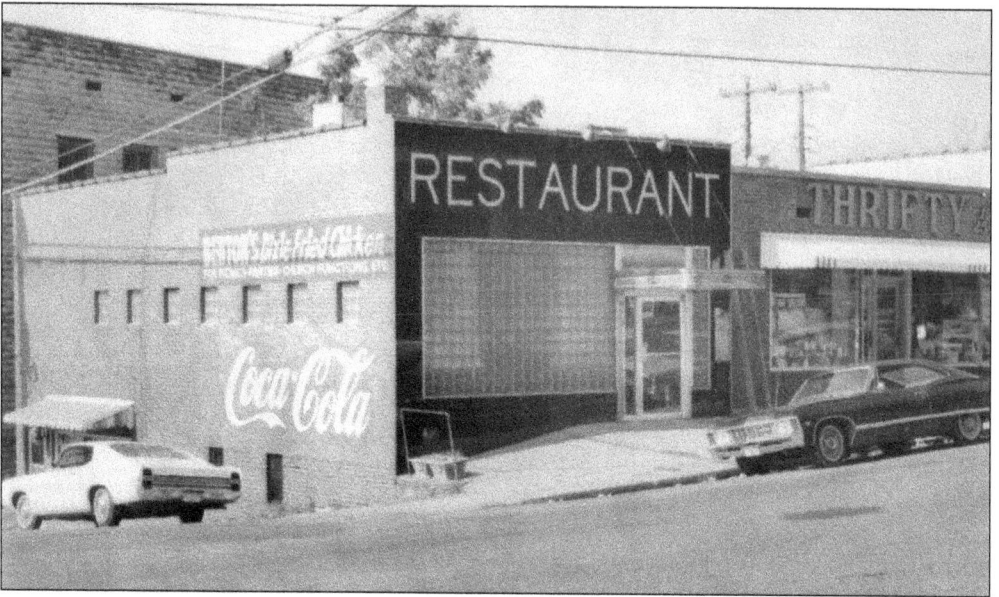

Facing east and north on the corner of Russell Avenue and Old Andrew Johnson Highway, this 1960s photograph shows the barbershop, the back of Minnis & Zirkle (later Park Belks and Keith's Department Store), Benton's Restaurant, and the Thrifty dime store. (Courtesy of Dennis Raper.)

Heading east on Old Andrew Johnson Highway in the late 1930s or early 1940s, downtown patrons shopped at Tallent's Drug Store and the various businesses in the Hinton Building. These included Pearl Haworth's dress shop and the Oriental Beauty Shop. Upstairs were dentists Drs. H.E. Hinton and W.P. Clear. Parked out front are a piano service car and the flower shop truck. Next door is the Flower Shop, Caldwell's Drugs, Jack Noe's Chrysler Plymouth dealership, the Esso gas station, and the Sinclair gas station, owned by Rolf Bell. (Courtesy of Juanita Franklin.)

Five

SERVICE WITH A SMILE
BUSINESSES

Several gristmills operated in Mossy Creek. This image appears to be of one of the earlier establishments. It was called the Branner/Jarnigan Mill and was located near Glenmore Mansion. It was later called the Jefferson City Milling Company and operated until 1951. The building was burned by vandals in 1964. (Courtesy of First United Methodist Church.)

MOSSY CREEK M'F'G. CO.

—————MANUFACTURE—————

V. B. SIZER, PRES.
J. C. JOHNSTON, MANG. & TREAS.
H. A. SIZER, SEC.
C. W. CATE, SUP'T.

(1)

Wooden Wash-boards, Pie and Biscuit Boards, Brackets, Mouldings, &c.

Mossy Creek, East Tenn., SEP 10 1892 189___

Dear Father: - Mr. Shepard has been here and left this A.M. I showed him all over the country and hope he was pleased with it, but as he did'nt express himself I am unable to say whether he was or was not pleased. The Harris house is for sale but not for rent if they can possibly sell it, so , so far as the house business is concerned, his trip was a failure. He came in rather unexpectedly Saturday morning but it gave him a chance to look around the plae by himself and form his own opinions.
We have got the bill for the machine and the machine too, but they didnot send the rollor for cross crimping and so as we have not got the money to pay for it, I notied them of the fact and tol them as soon as all of the machine was shipped we would send them a check for the amount. You can see them about it if you want to.
George, Will and myself are having the be a discussion as to wheth

S. E. RANKIN, President.   C. R. RANKIN, Sec. & Treas.

JEFFERSON CREAMERY,

MANUFACTURERS OF

BUTTER AND CHEESE.

Mossy Creek, Tenn Nov 7 189

Pictured are documents on stationery from two of Mossy Creek's businesses in the early 1890s. The Sizers and Rankins were both influential families in the community for many years. (Above, courtesy of Alice Pryor; at left, Cleve Smith.)

In the early 1900s, Edgar's store was operated by Tom and Bill Edgar. It was located on the north side of the railroad tracks on Depot Street. Dudley Northern operated from under the back of Edgar's and bought eggs, butter, and chickens from farmers, who then used the money to buy staples and other items from the store. The store burned and was later replaced by a yellow brick building that housed the Hull Wholesale Company. It was operated by brothers Clarence and Erwin Hull, who sold goods to stores for resale. The photograph below shows the interior of Edgar's general merchandise store. Pictured are Charlie Slover (left) and most likely one of the Edgar brothers behind the counter. (Above, Diamond Jubilee Bicentennial Celebration.)

The old Mossy Creek Bank was located on Depot Street, which later became Main Street. It stood above the sidewalk between two large trees, with stone steps leading up to the door. The bank failed during the Depression after the stock market crash of 1929. Later, First National Bank operated on the same site. (Courtesy of Helen Jolley.)

This is a financial report on the condition of Mossy Creek Bank at the end of 1911. With a slogan of "Safe, Sound, Solid, Conservative," it painted a more positive picture than what would unfortunately occur less than two decades later. (Courtesy of Cleve Smith.)

REPORT OF THE CONDITION OF

MOSSY CREEK BANK

OF

JEFFERSON CITY, TENN.

STATE DEPOSITORY

AS REPORTED TO THE COMPTROLLER OF THE TREASURY AT THE
CLOSE OF BUSINESS, DECEMBER 30, 1911

RESOURCES		LIABILITIES	
Loans and Discounts	$107,460.10	Capital Stock	$50,000.00
Overdrafts	1,787.51	Surplus	15,000.00
Banking House, Furniture and Fixtures	5,255.50	Undivided Profits, net	2,146.25
Stocks, Bonds and Securities	11,680.00	Deposits	76,408.24
		Bills Payable	NONE
CASH		Cashier's Checks (outstanding)	8.49
		Dividend Checks (outstanding)	10.00
Due from Banks	$12,301.36		
Checks and Cash Items	766.48		
Cash in Vault	4,322.03		
$143,572.98		**$143,572.98**	

We pay 4 per cent. per annum on deposits for three months, when
Certificates are issued for same. Safety Deposit Boxes for Rent.

We solicit your bank account.
Over $140,000.00 of solvent assets for the protection of depositors.
Fire Proof Vault, Burglar Proof Safe, Time Locks
Safe, Sound, Solid, Conservative

This building was used as a livery stable in the early days of Mossy Creek. R.M. Bales (in the 1890s), and later John R. Moser (around 1908), provided "taxi" service for the citizens of Mossy Creek. The horseshoe vent can be seen over the door. In the 1920s, the building was purchased by the Mossy Creek Canning Company. Later, the Stokley Cannery used it as a warehouse. The building is now owned by the Blanc & West Lumber Company and used as a warehouse. (Courtesy of Nancy Dalton.)

This 1900 receipt shows the funeral expenses for Samuel Rankin, with itemized expenses for transporting the casket. (Courtesy of Cleve Smith.)

Ralph Mountcastle was the founder and co-owner of the woolen mill. It was located on the north side of the railroad tracks on Mechanic Street, now Cherokee Drive. It had one of the first fire hoses in the city. In the early 1900s, it was sold to the Lockett family. The mill shut down and stood empty for a time until it was purchased by John E. Johnson, who operated the Johnson Spring Factory there for many years. (Courtesy of Ginger Burchett.)

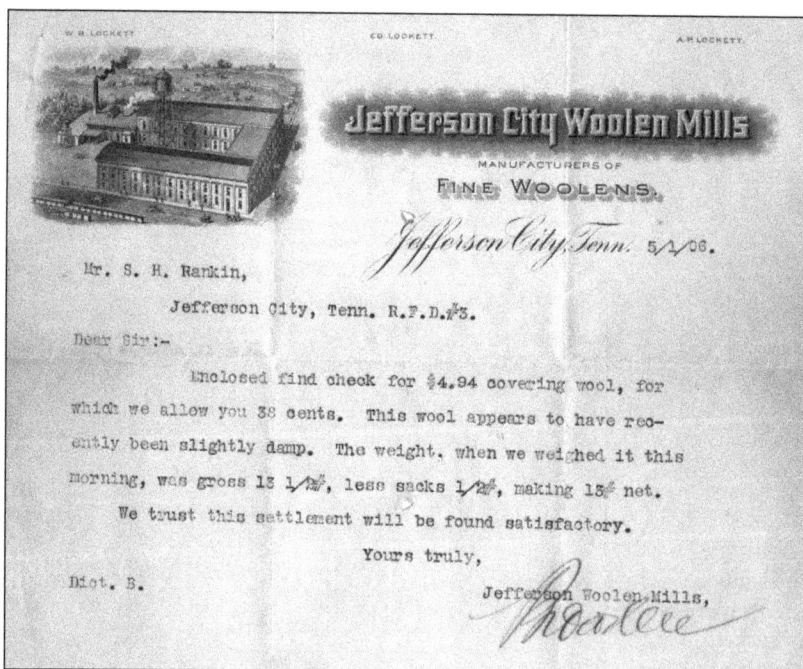

This 1906 receipt is from the Lockett family's days of ownership and details the payment of some "slightly damp wool." Note the drawing in the upper-left corner showing the addition of the southern wing. (Courtesy of Cleve Smith.)

Once painted red, these "Red Row" houses were built on Mechanic Street (present-day Cherokee Drive). There is uncertainty regarding their construction and whether the railroad built them for their employees or if they were constructed for the woolen mill workers. Later, they were occupied by Johnson Spring Factory workers. Needless to say, they offered shelter for those who could not afford something else. They were torn down in the late 1950s or early 1960s. (Courtesy of Helen Jolley.)

Knitting Mill Opens in Jefferson City, 1923

New Knitting Mill
Jefferson City, Feb. 12 -- W. A. Peck, the master mechanic of the Taubel-Scott, Kitzmiller Inc. of Riverside, N. J., and New York City, will have the new hosiery knitting mill plant in running operation by tomorrow.
Forty-seven loopers, 166 ribbers, and 103 machines and 4 large inspector's tables have been installed. There are a total of 255 machines already installed. They occupy two large rooms over the Nanny McCall Hardware Co., and one over the Jefferson City Post-office building.
Source: Grainger County News, 21 February 1923

This article from the February 21, 1923, Grainger County News gave citizens a glimpse into the workings of the latest industry to come to Jefferson City, which provided numerous jobs. (Courtesy of the Grainger County News.)

Jefferson City Grocery & Poultry Company (the "Poultry" was later dropped) was located on the north side of Depot Street, across from the Old Mossy Creek Bank. It advertised "prompt delivery service" and offered the "best prices for country produce."

Talley Bros. Confectionery was operated by Beecher Talley and sold tobacco, sweets, and, on Saturdays, ice cream. It was thought to be located on the street floor of the Yoe Hotel. In the photograph are Beecher Talley (left) and his younger brother Frank.

Pictured is the first motorized hearse in Jefferson City, but the operating funeral home is not identified. The first mortuary in town was purchased in 1912 from Cate Undertaking Company by W.J. Ore. Later, W.C. Taylor operated a funeral home on Branner Avenue. Upon the death of Taylor, the business was purchased by Roy Farrar in 1926. (Courtesy of Tennessee State Library and Archives.)

In 1911, the Mason Drug Company succeeded the Jefferson City Drug Company on Depot Street and with the collective history boasted that it was the "oldest drug store in town." By late 1912, it was renamed the Mason-Tarr Drug Company and was located in the Mason-Tarr building, opposite the depot. In December 1915, renovations created a new ice cream parlor in the store's rear and advertised as being "a nice, cozy place to meet your friends." Sometime during 1916, the business reverted to the original Mason Drug Company.

The old First National Bank had a brief life on the north side of Main Street. Another bank, Citizen's Trust Company, operated on the east end of Main Street for about 20 years. It consolidated with First National Bank and moved across the street to the site of the Old Mossy Creek Bank. (At left, courtesy of Tennessee State Library and Archives; below, Helen Jolley.)

Needing to expand, the bank purchased the Lloyd May Department Store building next door and completed renovations in the late 1950s. (Courtesy of Dennis Raper.)

The Jefferson Café sat beside the old Jefferson Theater on Main Street. Over the years, it had many owners and operators. It was advertised as "the home of that famous hamburger, coffee, and pies." Shown here is Hollis Talley, who worked at the café with his brother Beecher, who was the operator. The photograph is dated to 1936 or 1937.

Sam Massengill operated a shoe repair shop on Main Street. Then, in 1940, he moved his business to a small shop on Branner Avenue. He repaired shoes, belts, pocketbooks, and the like, sometimes while the customer waited. He is pictured with his first sewing machine. His big smile and singsong voice made his shop a favorite. (Courtesy of Tennessee State Library and Archives.)

The first barbershop in Jefferson City was owned by Louis Ingram and located on the northeast corner of Branner and Main Streets. Later, when Howard Ingram joined Louis, the barbershop moved across the street to the ground floor of the Yoe Hotel. It was called Ingram Bros. and also offered the cleaning and pressing of garments, as well as hot and cold baths. After World War II, Bill Tate bought an interest in the shop. It was known as Ingram & Tate and was moved across the street to the north side of Main Street. (Courtesy of Heritage Jefferson County.)

This Jefferson Pharmacy sat on the right side of Jefferson Hardware on Main Street. Drs. Albert Sydney Johnson and William "Bill" Kinder were pharmacists. It was known for its ice cream parlor in the back. Many a chocolate sundae, milk shake, or malt was made and served by Deloris Richardson or Frances Bowman.

These men are gathered in front of Albright's Drug Store, located to the left of the Jefferson Theater. The drugstore was owned by W.D. Albright, the first registered pharmacist in Jefferson City. He purchased it in 1920, and it was sold by his son in 1946 to Mrs. Hickey, who operated a café there. This 1921 photograph shows, from left to right, W.D. Albright, Charles A. Catlett, Zack Godwin, Humpy McElveen, Dr. B.M. Tittsworth, and Dr. R.M. McCown. (Courtesy of Betty Catlett.)

M .... $ ....
BILL TO DATE
Address ....
Salesman.................... Date...................... 191 5

L. A. TRENTHAM,
Groceries and Meats.
JEFFERSON CITY,   -   -   TENN.

Telephone 44.   Am't For'd $

1			60
2			40
3			13
4			15
5			1 18
6			
7			
8			
9			
10	19		

IN CASE OF ERROR PLEASE RETURN THIS BILL.
Re-Issued Pat. No. 12684, Mar. 20, '07. Mf'd by Amer. Sales Book Co., Ltd., Elmira N. Y

One of the first "modern" grocery stores, Trentham's was operated by Marshall Trentham. It provided delivery service in addition to walk-in service. It was located in what would later become, along with several nearby buildings, the Leeper Hardware Company. Seen above inside Trentham's are, from left to right, owner Marshall Trentham, Joe Miles, and Hollis Talley. The 1915 receipt at left shows Sam Rankin's "on the way home from work" shopping list. (At left, courtesy of Cleve Smith.)

Mack Epps operated a cabstand on the corner of Russell Avenue and Main Street in what was later the Franklin Super Market lower parking lot. There were other cab services, including Denton's, "Tweetie" Miller's, and later Gann's. (Courtesy of Juanita Franklin.)

W.G. Shipe built Shipe Hardware in 1940. In 1946, Bill Catlett became a partner and it was renamed Shipe & Catlett Hardware. In 1956, Charles "Buddy" Catlett bought into the business. Many a tall tale has been told around the potbellied coal stove that sat in the middle of the store. Buddy's son Chuck and his wife became owners in 2000 and moved it to Highway 11E. The business was closed in 2009. (Courtesy of Betty Catlett.)

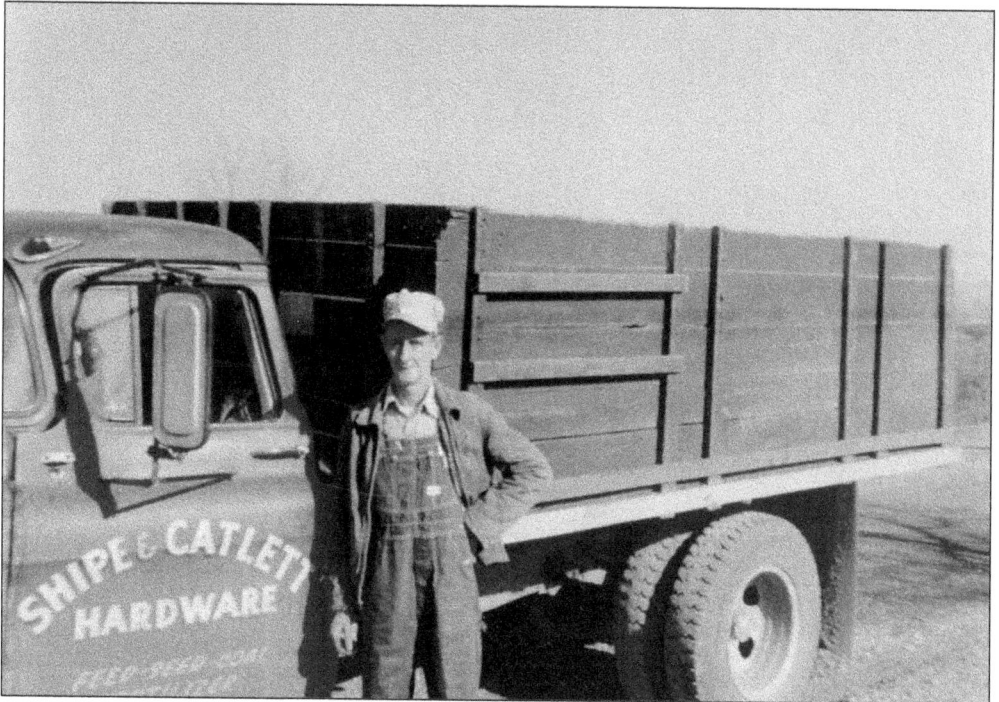

John Talley was just one of the men who worked for Shipe & Catlett driving the coal trucks. Their trucks hauled coal from Kentucky to the store and then made deliveries to homes and businesses. (Courtesy of Ann Acuff.)

The Johnson Spring Factory, Inc., was founded by Finland native John Emil Johnson and his son Roy Daniel Johnson. Johnson bought the former woolen mill and later found out the deal included the 10 small houses known as Red Row. For many years, he rented the houses to employees. The company made springs for chairs, sofas, mattresses, and box springs and held a patent on the Johnson Easel, a popular item with florists. At one time, the business employed over 200 people. Roy took over as president when his father became disabled. Later, he and his son Danny operated the plant until it was sold to the Steadly Company in 1982. (Courtesy of Janie Talley Gass.)

Heartiest congratulations to athletic mine employees for an outstanding safety record of working 122,549 man hours without a lost time injury since June 26, 1946.

M. J. Langley
January 1, 1949

In 1949, Athletic Mine employees smile about their safety record. Pictured are, from left to right, (first row) Eli Carter, J.C. Brinkley, Frank Anderson, Walt McMillan, Luke Stills, Joe Cox, and Hobart Anderson; (second row) Fred Thurman, Hugh Paul Russell, Bob Climer, Theodore Roach, Harold Lowery, Carl Cain, Jack Kellog, Dave Newman, Raymond Hayworth, Lee Ramsey, Joe Myers, and Arthur Allen (geologist). (Courtesy of Cleve Smith.)

The Hinton Building was constructed in the mid-1930s for Dr. H.E. Hinton and his wife. He had a dentist office upstairs and rented the downstairs to various businesses. These included the Fashion Shop, owned by Pearl and Mae Haworth, the Oriental Beauty Shop, owned by Bernice Shipley, J.E. Wardrip Insurance, Neil Manley Real Estate, and Southern Securities. In 1973, after Dr. Hinton passed away, Hugh and Clara Cate bought the building. Cate had an insurance business and started a radio station, WSBM. The Cates sold the building in 1981 to Ken Klinger and James B. Mimbs of Florida, who bought the building and radio station from Klinger. Art and Marty Dees bought the radio station in 1985. Don Cochran purchased the building after it stood empty for a time, and his son Nick operated Jefferson Printing Company. After it went out of business, the building was bought by Spencer and Libby Jones. With the help of business majors at Carson-Newman, Jones remodeled, designed, and built the current business, The Creek, a sandwich, ice cream, and coffee shop. (Above, courtesy of Cleve Smith; below, Dennis Raper.)

Franklin Super Market was once used as a state maintenance building. It was bought in the 1930s by W.G. Shipe and became a grocery store. The store was later sold to C.R. and Chester Franklin, who changed the name to Franklin's Super Market. Later, it was Franklin's IGA Supermarket. The upper floor was once used as a boxing arena. The Odd Fellows met there for a time, and C.R. Franklin, his wife, Julia, and his mother also lived there. The store went out of business in the late 1970s, and the building was bought by Buddy Catlett. He remodeled the downstairs for several businesses and the upstairs into a loft apartment.

Hollis Talley began working for Grady Shipe in 1940. He became manager at Franklin's and worked there until his retirement in 1976. Many area high school and college men remember working for him as "bag boys."

Leeper Hardware is prepared for Christmas in this 1950s photograph, showing off its selection of bicycles. Its original location was on East Main Street before R.J. Leeper relocated to Highway 11E. He set up business in buildings that three other stores and the old post office had occupied. (Courtesy of Lisa Williams.)

In the 1950s, Jessie Slover operated a dress shop in the Lambdin Building, located on the east end of Main Street. Later, Helen Northern bought the business and called it Helen's Dress Shop. (Courtesy of Dennis Raper.)

Carl Skeen, the son of Hubert Skeen, built his furniture company on Andrew Johnson Highway in 1946. His father owned Skeen Furniture Store on Main Street. Carl retired in 1986 and died in 1990. His son Clifford and his wife later operated the store. Carl was also a land developer, building several area subdivisions and rental properties. His family continues to run the Skeen Rental Agency. (Courtesy of Dennis Raper.)

The *Jefferson City Standard* was first published in 1929. In 1956, it was purchased from Judge George Shepherd by Tom Gentry (seated), along with the *Dandridge Banner* and the *Grainger County News*. In 1965, he consolidated the Dandridge and Jefferson City papers into the *Jefferson County Standard Banner*. A World War II Navy veteran and cattleman as well as publisher, Gentry provided news for the community for over 50 years. Tom's son Dale (standing) is the current owner and editor. It is published each Tuesday and Thursday and has a combined circulation of 14,000. (Courtesy of Dave Gentry.)

In 1936, O.W. Farris (below, left) came to Jefferson City and opened a service station and repair shop. In 1941, he became a Desoto Plymouth dealer. His son Johnny O. Farris joined him in 1945. They moved to a larger dealership in 1947. They became a Chrysler Plymouth dealership in 1960, and O.W.'s grandson Johnny Wayne Farris joined them in 1972. In 1977, they built their present location on Highway 11E. O.W. Farris died in 1983, and Johnny O. died in 1988. Johnny Wayne Farris continues to own and operate the business. (Above, courtesy of Dennis Raper; below, courtesy of Nancy Farris.)

Six

SPIRITUAL FOUNDATIONS
CHURCHES

Soon after arriving, Mossy Creek's first settlers, Adam and Elizabeth Peck, built a log structure later known as the First Methodist Meeting House on Mossy Creek. In 1850, the first church building was constructed on Peck land, near what is now the old part of Westview Cemetery, and named Elizabeth's Chapel. Presbyterians and Methodists worshiped together there for many years. During the Civil War, Union soldiers used the chapel as a hospital. After much discussion, church trustees purchased two lots on May 10, 1884. In 1887, the church moved into its new white frame building at the corner of Church Street and Branner Avenue and became Mossy Creek Methodist Church, using some of the lumber and windowsills from the old church. In 1939, they officially adopted the name First Methodist Church. (Courtesy of First United Methodist Church.)

Top row: O. E. Godwin, R. W. Manley, Frank Taylor, Walter Cowan, J. C. Galbraith, W. O. Brimer, Bob Purkey, Shell Emert, Tom Edgar, Ed Cates, W. H. Lockhart, W. T. Peck, Bob Rector, J. H. Belk, Frank Slover, Lon Finley, Ben Cowan, J. R. Shipley, Will Franklin and J.E. Easley.

Second row: Will Kite, Ernest Davis, Marshall Trentham, C.M. McMahan, Artie Lowe, Arlie Hickman, Dr. R. M. McCown, teacher; B. B. Roach, Forrest Garrett, Sherman Brown, Charles Miller, and F. A. Talley.

Third row: Jesse James, W. H. Kinder, Robert Lowe, Horace Hurst, John Seaton, Otis Wright, Frank Mullendore, Paul Hudson, W. A. Edgar and Jerry Nelson.

Fourth Row: Will Godwin, Harley Hurst, Howard Edgar, Zack Godwin, W. D. Albright, John Hoosier.

In 1901, when Mossy Creek was renamed Jefferson City, the Methodist Episcopal Church, South, was the only white Methodist church in Jefferson City. George Timmons was a member of the First United Methodist Church, where he was Sunday school superintendent in the early 1900s and taught a men's Sunday school class. Dr. R.M. McCown also taught a large men's Sunday school class and was known for his interpretations of the Bible. (Courtesy of First United Methodist Church.)

The church was remodeled in 1957 and again in 1984. In 1998, another refurbishing was completed. The church bought adjoining property and currently owns the entire block. (Courtesy of Ronnie Housely.)

Around 1870, the first recorded meetings of Martha Davis Baptist Church were in a blacksmith shop located in Mossy Creek, adjacent to the Jarnigan Mill. The church was named in honor of Martha Davis, who had lived in Tazewell before moving to Jefferson City. In 1879, with her help, members were able to construct the church building that stands today. The church is known as "the little church on the hill, with its doors opened to all who wish to enter." The congregation celebrated their 135th anniversary in October 2013. (Courtesy of Beverly Phipps.)

For many years, Martha Davis has had an active youth and young adult choir. They would regularly help lead worship, singing during services on the third Sunday of each month. (Courtesy of Beverly Phipps.)

Boyd Chapel traces its roots from the first meetinghouse in Mossy Creek and Elizabeth's Chapel. Later, in 1867, a log building known as the Methodist Episcopal Church was built on Odell Lane on land given by John Roper Branner for a church, school, and cemetery for the African American citizens of Jefferson County. In 1889, a wooden structure was completed on the hill overlooking Mossy Creek and named Boyd Chapel Methodist Episcopal Church. The land was sold to the trustees of the church for $25.

A parade of Masons in regalia from Jefferson City and Alcoa was held to lay the cornerstone. The present red-brick structure was built in the front yard of the original wooden structure. (Courtesy of Tennessee State Library and Archives.)

Seen here are Sunday morning worshippers, with George Peck seated in the second row on the left. (Courtesy of the Peck family.)

Having met previously with the Methodists at Elizabeth's Chapel, Presbyterians organized in 1867 as Mossy Creek Presbyterian Church, with 49 members, five ruling elders, and three deacons. They empowered trustees S.N. Fain, R.H. Ashmore, and W.M. Newman to buy land from the Branner estate. Building began in 1869. A violent storm blew the walls down in 1871 just as they were preparing to put the roof on the structure. Rebuilding began right away, and on December 16, 1871, the "house was finished." The church continued to buy surrounding land, and a manse was built. In 1880, the Ladies Aid Society got enough money together to purchase a bell for the belfry, which remains today.

The building that houses George Street United Methodist Church was constructed in 1887. On August 26, 1907, the Methodist Episcopal Church bought the building and property from the First Baptist Church of Jefferson City for $1,300. It was then called Second Methodist Church of Jefferson City until the name was changed to George Street Methodist Church.

The First Baptist Church's history is traced back to the Mossy Creek Baptist Church, which was a merger of the Black Oak Grove and Oakland Churches. The move to Mossy Creek took place on May 8, 1841. The first building was located on the west bank of Mossy Creek near the zinc mines. It was demolished during the Civil War. The church relocated to what was known as Carsonville in 1881 in what is now known as the George Street United Methodist Church. In 1909, the church built on its present Russell Avenue location. With the money the government repaid for damages to the original building, the church bought a pipe organ. In 1938, D.L. Butler gave the money for an educational building. In the early 1960s, a new building was constructed and dedicated. (Courtesy of Juanita Franklin.)

In December 1962, during a college chapel service, the south side of the balcony fell as the student body stood to sing the "Hallelujah Chorus." It was repaired, and the church thrived until December 2, 1985, when the church caught fire, destroying the sanctuary and damaging the educational building and offices. For 12 hours, 70 firefighters from five areas battled the fire. Church services were relocated to Carson-Newman's Gentry Auditorium, located in the Henderson Humanities Building. (Above, photograph by Chet Brogan; below, courtesy of Patrick Gass.)

Rebuilding began in early 1987, and the present sanctuary was dedicated on May 29, 1988, featuring the 9-foot-by-18-foot *Christ and the Children* stained-glass window. Designed by Elizabeth Mask, the window was a gift of Lady Kate Catlett and family friends in memory of her husband, William Catlett.

The first East Tennessee Baptist Preachers' School held at Carson-Newman was a joint effort with the Tennessee Baptist Convention's education department. Organized by Pres. J.T. Warren and Dr. A.F. Mahan, it ran for four weeks. The school became an annual affair, with many pastors coming each year. The first women's class was started in 1942 and ran until 1999.

Emmanuel Baptist Church began as White Zion Church. In 1902, the church was organized as Second Baptist Church of Jefferson City. In 1922, the name was changed to Northside Baptist Church. A new structure was built, and by 1936 the church was free of building debt. The church soon realized it would need extra space, and in 1955 lots were purchased on Overlook Avenue with the idea of building and relocating when needed. After moving to the west side of the city in 1969, the church voted to change its name to Emmanuel Baptist Church.

"SET FOR THE DEFENSE OF THE GOSPEL."

This is to Certify, that after a satisfactory relation of his Christian experience, call to the Ministry, and views of Bible doctrine,

J. A. Lockhart.

was publicly ordained to the work of

The Gospel Ministry,

on the _12_ day of _Nov._ 1899, by a Council of Baptist Churches, composed of_____ messengers from_____ churches, convened at the call of the _Flat Gap_ Church at _New Market, Tenn_

J. M. Phillips Moderator.

J. M. Burnett Clerk.

J. M. Oley

L. Cooper

Other smaller churches in and around the city were served by circuit-rider preachers. These men traveled from church to church preaching only one or two sermons per month at each church. Jesse Archibald Lockhart was born on August 24, 1871, in the Flat Gap Community in Jefferson County. He began his ministry in 1896, with his first pastorate at Pleasant View in 1899. By the time he retired in 1946, he had pastored at 32 different churches in Jefferson, Grainger, Hamblen, Greene, Sevier, and Knox Counties and served in Cumberland Gap, Kentucky. (Courtesy of Opalee Queen.)

Seven

MEETING A COMMUNITY'S NEEDS
CITY SERVICES

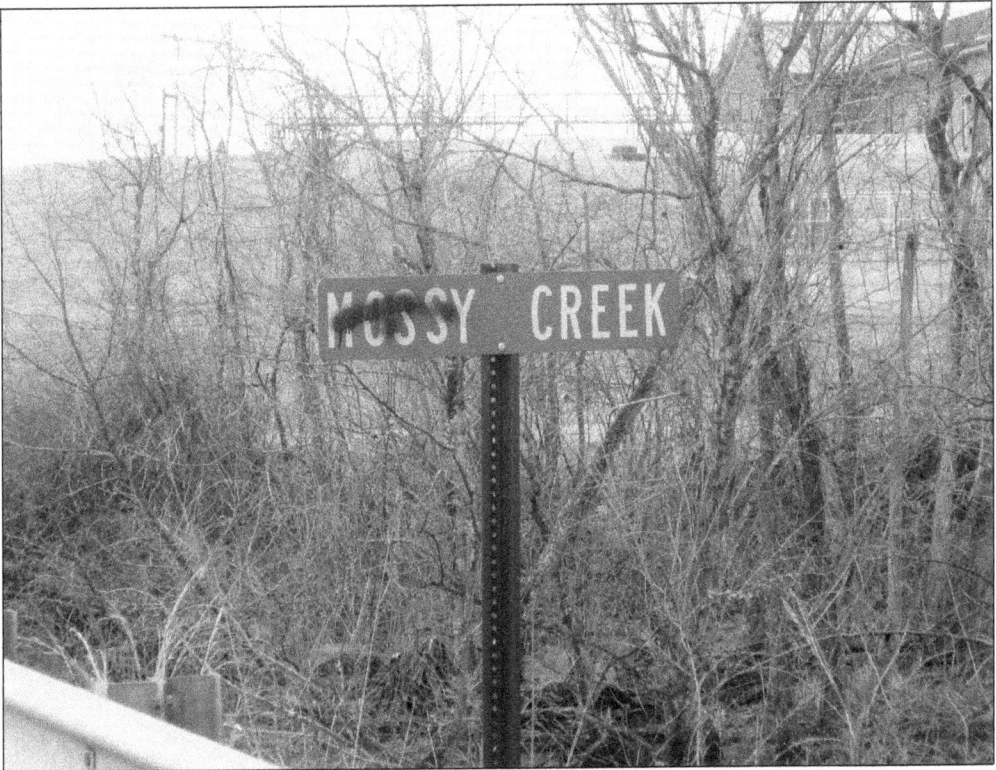

The Mossy Creek sign is located on the south side of Highway 11E heading east. In the background is the new water treatment facility, completed in 2013. The creek is fed by a spring directly behind the plant and produces close to 1.5 million gallons of water a day. Combined with the three million gallons produced daily by the Jarnigan mine, water is provided for Jefferson City, New Market, and the Shady Grove community.

The first United States post office was located at the Mossy Creek Iron Works in 1816, with Willie Blount Peck as the postmaster. Other postmasters were William Brazelton, Christopher Hanes, George Branner, John R. Branner, James Ashmore, James Watkins, Ambrose Witt, and Burgess Witt. In 1901, the post office name was changed to Jefferson City. Joseph Ellis, Frank Gilbreath, Ira Marshall Coile, Luke C. Peak, and Tom Edgar served as postmasters. Located on Branner Avenue for a time, it later occupied two locations on Main Street. (Above, Diamond Jubilee Bicentennial Celebration; at left, Cleve Smith.)

In August 1940, the new post office, located on Andrew Johnson Highway, was dedicated. Ralph Keith Godwin was postmaster at the time. After his death in 1947, his wife, Iva M. Godwin, was appointed to fill his position. She served until her retirement in 1968, and William Swann was appointed her successor. (Courtesy of Juanita Franklin.)

The US government got into the art business when it instituted a series of programs to keep artists working during the Depression years. Artists competed for the job of painting murals in 1,100 post offices throughout the nation. Tennessee has 30 such murals in post offices throughout the state. The Jefferson City mural was painted by Charles Child of Pennsylvania and was installed in 1941. It is entitled *Great Smokies and Tennessee Farms*.

John Roper Branner provided the land for the East Tennessee & Virginia Railroad Company to come through Mossy Creek as it completed its new route in 1858 connecting Knoxville and Bristol. Branner stipulated that all passenger trains must stop in Mossy Creek. (Courtesy of Tennessee State Library and Archives.)

The first building, completed in 1870, burned in 1930, and a new building was erected later that same year. (Courtesy of Tennessee State Library and Archives.)

In 1985, the Southern Railroad petitioned the city to move the depot back five feet from its right-of-way. The city elected not to incur the expense. After valiant efforts to save the building, it was torn down in 1987. (Above, courtesy of Barbara Peck Dean; below, Susie Blanc Jarnagin and Ronnie Housely.)

In 1868, John Roper Branner deeded four lots to the Masonic lodge to build on. The first floor of the building was used for a school and the second floor for the lodge. In 1904, the city was given half of the property, and the city government occupied the first floor. In 1930, the building was divided and partitioned off. The original building was remodeled, and a wing was later added. City government offices utilized this building until 1989, when they moved to the former Estes Funeral Home on Andrew Johnson Highway.

OFFICIAL BALLOT

FOR THE

MUNICIPAL ELECTION
JEFFERSON CITY,

Jefferson County, Tennessee

ELECTION, MAY 4, 1905

FOR

MAYOR AND ALDERMEN

Pictured is an early Jefferson City municipal election ballot for mayor and alderman. The mayoral election was won by Herbert S. Butterworth. He defeated Robert M. "Bob" Bales, who had served two consecutive terms. (Courtesy of Alice Pryor.)

Clyde Pike, who was later the mayor of Jefferson City, stands beside a city maintenance truck. (Courtesy of Dennis Raper.)

The first known mechanized fire engine was a converted 1927 Buick automobile. Note the ladders on makeshift side hooks. (Courtesy of Betty Catlett.)

In the 1930s, Margaret Justice, RN, oversaw the hospital on Jefferson Street, leasing the building from Dr. R.M. McCown. The space quickly became too small, and another facility was erected next door. Drs. Clark Fain and Frank Milligan joined Dr. McCown in the practice. In 1947, Dr. Milligan opened Milligan Clinic and was joined by Dr. E.P. Muncy. The old Jefferson Hospital closed about that time, but within a year Justice reopened Jefferson Hospital in a stone house on Russell Avenue where Drs. Fain, McCown, Eugene Howard, and John Ellis practiced. In 1960, a new Hill Burton Hospital opened on Bishop Avenue. In 1996, it was sold to St. Mary's Health System. With the construction of the new hospital, the old facility was sold to Carson-Newman. (Courtesy of Dennis Raper.)

Farrar Funeral Home's history dates back to 1924, when family members purchased the Bill Ore Undertaking Company, changing its name to the W.C. Taylor Undertaking Company. Located on Main Street next to the Ingram Barber Shop, it remained there until moving to May Manor in the 1930s. Due to increasing need for space, the business moved to Russell Avenue. When Roy E. Farrar Sr. obtained complete interest in 1942, the company changed to its current name. In 1974, the funeral home moved to its present location on Broadway Boulevard, and it is still operated by the Farrar family.

September 1, 1940, proved a landmark day in Jefferson County, as the Appalachian Electric Cooperative began operations. The first move came in 1951, when it moved the headquarters down Old Andrew Johnson Highway to what would be its home for the next 45 years. In the 1960s, an addition was added to the main building, and new substations were added throughout the county. Underground lines began to be laid in the 1970s, and computerization started in 1975. The New Market operation center opened in 1980, and more efficient technology was continually added, along with more substations. Since 1940, AEC has grown from 6 employees to over 90 and increased its lines from 243 miles to over 2,600. (Both courtesy of Appalachian Electric Cooperative.)

Eight

ARCHITECTURAL JEWELS
HISTORIC HOMES

In 1899, friends and members of the Sizer family enjoy boating on Mossy Creek below the front yard of the family home, known as Seven Gables. (Courtesy of Helen Jolley.)

This house was built in 1875 by Col. Sam Fain, a wealthy merchant, cotton-thread mill owner, and land speculator. The house had solid walls, using almost 180,000 bricks. In 1925, it was modernized at a cost of $6,000, with electricity and running water added. The house had a slate roof, white oak flooring, and walnut and chestnut woodwork. There were six rooms downstairs, five bedrooms and three baths upstairs, and six cedar-lined closets. In 1941, the land was condemned and taken by the Tennessee Valley Authority to be flooded by the construction of Cherokee Dam. After a bitter court battle, John R. Fain, the son of Samuel and the owner at the time, was awarded $35,500 for the house and the land. The house was torn down, and the land is now under water. (Courtesy of John Fain.)

Standing on the log cabin site of Jefferson City's first settler, Adam Peck, Thomas Tittsworth built this house in 1842 with bricks made on-site by slaves. After his death, the house went to his son Dr. Isaac M. Tittsworth, a graduate of the University of Nashville (now Vanderbilt Medical School). He practiced medicine in Mossy Creek until his death in 1908. He built a house in town and gave the former house to his son Harry, who built a new house across the road and used the original home as a tenant house. In the 1940s, many of the neighboring homes and farms were claimed by the Tennessee Valley Authority for the construction of Cherokee Dam. This house was spared, and in the 1950s TVA deeded it to Jefferson City, and it was used as a community center and boys' club. It was later destroyed by fire. (Above, E.P. Muncy, *People and Places of Jefferson County*.)

This Reconstruction-era Italianate mansion, known as Hampton Hall or the Longmire House, is located on part of the original land grant of town founders Adam and Elizabeth Peck. Thomas Tittsworth started the house at the beginning of the Civil War but died in 1863. The house was later completed by Joseph Branner, the son of John Roper Branner, in 1872. Several families have owned the property, including Thomas Cowan from 1807 until 1946, followed by the Longmire family, who resided there until 1989. The property was purchased that year by the Durmans, who operate an organic farm there, raising fruits and heirloom vegetables.

In 1850, farmer and livestock trader Stokely Williams hired well-known architect William Strickland, the designer of the Tennessee State Capitol, to design a home on the Mossy Creek to Morristown road for he and his wife, Mary P. Reese. Mary planted the gardens around the house. During the Civil War, the house was used as a hospital, and soldiers were buried in the gardens. The War Department disinterred the soldiers to a more suitable burial ground in 1912. Lizzie Read James bought Fairview in 1880, and members of the James family have lived there ever since. The house, in the Greek Revival style, was added to the National Register of Historic Places in 1982. The current occupants are Larry and Mary Evelyn (James) Musick. Pictured below around 1885 on the porch are Samuel and Elizabeth "Lizzie" Read James and members of their family. (Both courtesy of Mary Evelyn Musick.)

Designed and built by William S. Sizer, Seven Gables sits on a hillside gently sloping down to Mossy Creek. He was a partner and superintendent of Wadsworth Sizer Paint Company in New Jersey. In 1866, he was sent by New York investors to Mossy Creek to purchase property and organize a zinc mining operation. The East Tennessee Zinc Company was formed for the manufacturing of oxide of zinc and spelter (metallic zinc) in Tennessee. The house was completed in 1867 at a cost of $10,000. The mines closed in 1871 due to investor financial issues. Sizer then began the Mossy Creek Manufacturing Company but later returned to the paint business. He died in 1892 at the home of his sister while on a business trip to Toledo, Ohio. (Courtesy of Helen Jolley.)

Pictured sitting in the yard of Seven Gables are owners William S. and Maria Sizer, with their daughter Helen Sizer (Moser) standing between them. Members of the family have continued to live in the house, down to its current owner, Helen Iddins Jolley. (Courtesy of Helen Jolley.)

Ownership of the land connected to this home can be traced to Christopher Haynes prior to 1772. In 1834, George Branner bought 706 acres and increased the property to about 1,500 acres. Upon his death in 1847, the estate was divided among his 10 children. Benjamin Manassus Branner added to his portion and built the house in the mid-1850s. The Branner family sold the property to Alfred R. Swann in the late 19th century, and he eventually gave it to his daughter Mrs. Lamar Rankin as a wedding present. They operated the farm until 1970, when the heirs auctioned off the house and 300 acres. Harold and Polly Hicks bought the house and 10 acres, while developers bought the remaining acreage. Polly Hicks restored the home and now operates it as a bed-and-breakfast. (Diamond Jubilee Bicentennial Celebration.)

This large Victorian-style home was built in 1871 by A.J. Mountcastle, a successful businessman and real estate agent. In 1876, the Mossy Creek Baptist College trustees purchased the 35-acre estate, which Highway 11E now runs through.

The property was sold to Jefferson City in 1917 and used for an elementary school. Carpenter and businessman Luther Beeler bought the house in 1922, followed by Mr. and Mrs. S.H. Rankin, who purchased it in 1930. Mrs. Rankin sold it to area Exxon distributor Rogers Petroleum, Inc., of Morristown in 1986. The mansion was finally razed in 1987, and another piece of Jefferson City history was lost to development. (Courtesy of Vic Pedone.)

Five Chimneys was built by Samuel I. Newman in 1840. He married Mary Ann Elmore, and they raised 12 children in the large home located on Flat Gap Road. It was later owned by Nelle and Lily Franklin. It changed owners several times and was placed in the National Register of Historic Places in 1978. In 2004, the house was sold for $187,500 to real estate developers the Ryan Company. Valiant attempts were made to raise the estimated $400,000 it would take to move the house to another property, but it was ultimately torn down. (Courtesy of Helen Gray.)

John Roper Branner built the house he called The Oaks in 1868–1869 but died before its completion. His brother Joseph lived there and operated the Branner Institute for Young Women in the 1870s. In 1882, Milton Preston Jarnagin bought the mansion, naming it Glenmore in memory of his son Glenmore Murrell Jarnagin, who died in infancy. After Jarnagin's death in 1895, his descendants continued to own Glenmore until the death of Frank Watkins Jarnagin. In 1970, the 12 Jarnagin heirs gave the home to the Association for the Preservation of Tennessee Antiquities (APTA). Due to the efforts of the Jefferson County APTA, the house was added to the National Register of Historic Places in 1973 and is maintained by the Jefferson County Historical Society.

Nine

TEACHING THE
NEXT GENERATION
EDUCATION

In 1858, Robert Reedy Bryan bought land and built a log cabin schoolhouse, where he taught young children, including 11 of his own, next to his home. In 1980, the structure was almost lost when a bulldozer was clearing the property for new construction. With the efforts of Helen Gray, the Jefferson County Historical Society, and the Association for the Preservation of Tennessee Antiquities, enough money was raised to move the structure to its present location on the crest of a hill between Jefferson Elementary and Middle Schools. Badly in need of restoration, the efforts of many were rewarded as new logs were located. The county commission allocated $13,000 for the work, and combined with $7,000 raised by the historical society the schoolhouse was dedicated to be used as a living history display for students in November 2011.

Rev. Peter Guinn, pastor of Martha Davis Baptist Church, helped secure the funds to purchase the land for a school in 1890. Two buildings were erected, and the school operated as an elementary and secondary school, with teacher training emphasized. Pictured below are Nelson Merry School faculty members from 1917 to 1920. They are, from left to right, (first row) Rev. J.M. Thompson, BTh (president, political economy, ethics, and Bible), Dr. C.C. Floyd (principal, algebra, geometry, and physiology), and professor W.S. Mitchell (normal preparatory, mathematics, and Latin); (second row) Margarete Harris (history and geography), Mrs. A.C. Thompson (English and Rhetoric), Lillian P. Murray (third and fourth grades), Fannie M. Jackson (not pictured, primary department and domestic arts), professor T.W. Austin (instrumental music and voice culture), and Mrs. B.V. Thompson (general preceptress). (Courtesy of Tennessee State Library and Archives.)

In 1932, the school was sold to Jefferson County and became the first African American public school. In 1956, Eugene Peck was principal, and during his tenure a gymnasium and science rooms were built. In 1965, the school was closed due to integration. (Courtesy of the Peck family.)

In 1868, John R. Branner deeded four lots to Mossy Creek Masonic Lodge No. 333 to be used for educational purposes. In 1904, the Masonic hall deeded half-interest to the city. City government occupied the first floor and the first public school was on the second floor. (Courtesy of Cleve Smith.)

Carson-Newman University had its origins in the early 1840s, when a number of Baptist leaders dreamed of an educational institution that eventually opened its doors in the fall of 1851 as Mossy Creek Missionary Baptist Seminary. The school would change names to Mossy Creek Baptist College in 1855, Carson College in 1880, and then Carson-Newman College in 1889 after joining with the female Newman College. The change to "University" came in 2013. Steeped in the ideals of truth, beauty, and goodness, the school has prepared students academically and spiritually for over 160 years.

In 1920, students in grades 1–12 moved into the new school, which was built on land purchased from Carson-Newman College. In 1926, a new high school was built. This school later became the lower elementary school when grades six through eight moved to the site of the old high school. A new elementary school was built in 1958 near the site of the new high school on Highway 11E. It housed kindergarten through eighth grade until 1975, when students in grades seven and eight moved to the former high school site nearby and it became Jefferson Middle School. The elementary school built in 1958 is still in use today, serving kindergarten through fifth grade. At right is Mrs. J.R. Moser's contract for the 1926–1927 school year. (Above, courtesy of Dennis Raper; below, Alice Pryor.)

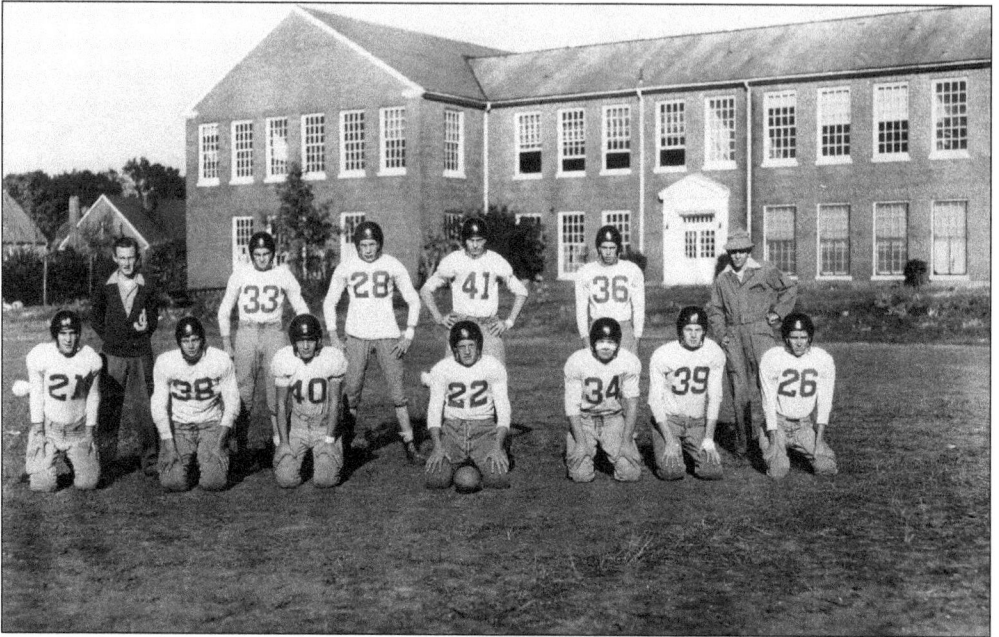

Pictured in front of the old Jefferson City High School, built in 1926 on Jefferson Street, is a 1930s football team; James Gass, the co-author's brother-in-law, is no. 33.

This building became the Upper Elementary School in 1951, when the new high school was erected on Highway 11E. (Courtesy of Juanita Franklin.)

The first high school was built in 1926 on a site beside the current swimming pool. It remained there until 1951, when a new high school was built on Highway 11E and grades six through eight moved into the building, then called the Upper Elementary School. It was later used as a recreation center until it burned. The city swimming pool and Little League field now occupy that site. In 1975, a new consolidated county high school was built on Highway 92, and the old high school became the middle school. (Courtesy of Juanita Franklin.)

A football team from Jefferson County High School, located on Highway 11E, is seen here in the 1950s. The coaches are Vernon Caldwell (left) and Jack Wade (right). (Courtesy of Betty Catlett.)

As Jefferson City's population grew, so did the need for larger schools. Elementary-age children in grades one through eight were split into lower and upper schools. In 1957, work began on a consolidated school, which opened the following year. In 1963, an addition was constructed. The school currently serves 600 students.

On April 6, 1992, Barnaby's Backyard was officially opened as an additional playground for Jefferson Elementary students. Featuring various swings, slides, climbing areas, and hiding places, it has provided wonderful memories for countless children. It is graciously maintained by the Rotary Club.

Ten

A COMMUNITY AT PLAY

RECREATION

With the construction of the dam by TVA in 1940 came the formation of Cherokee Lake, providing excellent recreational resources, including swimming, boating, fishing, and sailing. There is a large picnic area for day use and a small campground that is open during the warmer months.

Pictured are two baseball teams sponsored by local businesses. Above is the Jefferson City Zinc Company team. Below is a 1930s or 1940s photograph of the Spring Factory team, which included, from left to right, (first row) Frank Kelley, H.K. Horner, Robert Purkey, Jack Leonard, Milburne Line, Raymond Hurst, Fred Kelley, and I.F. Kelley; (standing) Adam Horner, Ott Nelson, Jim Long, Joe Miles, Deotis Haun, Claude Love, and Harry Carmichael. (Above, courtesy of Tennessee State Library and Archives; below, Barbara Parker.)

Dr. W.D. Albright built this tennis court for the youth of the community. (Courtesy of Betty Catlett.)

Jefferson City's first swimming pool opened on June 1, 1935, on private property owned by Dr. Albright. Open to the public, admission was 25¢ for adults and 15¢ for children. It used treated city water and was operated by coach Sam B. Frosty Holt. The pool was 50 feet long, 40 feet wide, and six feet, seven inches deep. In the 1960s, the local civic clubs built the city pool on the corner of Russell Avenue and West Jefferson Street, which is still in use today. (Courtesy of Betty Catlett.)

Jefferson City swimming has had a long and successful history. The early team members at left are, from left to right, Sandra Hallen, Danny Johnson, and Libby Hudson. The group of 1980s swimmers below proudly shows off its trophy. (At Left, courtesy of Libby Gardner; below, *Jefferson Standard Banner*.)

This team, coached by Charles A. "Buddy" Catlett, included, from left to right, (first row) Johnny Bill Hudson, Dean Collins, Jim Moyers, Bart Seals, and Bill Clark; (second row) Catlett, Bennie Collins, Jackie Case, Sam Hinchey, unidentified, David Skeen, and Clifford Skeen. (Courtesy of Betty Catlett.)

Participating in the American Legion tennis tournament awards presentation are, from left to right, Ken Kooch, Terrell Travis, Frank Ellis, coach J.O. Conwell, unidentified, Clark Sorrells, and Chuck Catlett. (Courtesy of Betty Catlett.)

These ladies bowled together for many years, and their team included, from left to right, Lady Kate Catlett, Lynette High, Polly Clear, Gwen Gass, and Helen Tarr. (Courtesy of Betty Catlett.)

Radio station WJFC sponsored a softball league for women. The coaches were Bruce Burgess, Keith Craig, Bill Talley, and Bill Tullock. Shown in this photograph are members of Bill Tullock's team. They are, from left to right, (first row) Joyce Dearstone, Nancy Tullock, unidentified, Rosa Kinder, and Libby Hudson; (second row) Adele Palmari, Sybil Smith, Bill Tullock, and Mary Weems. (Courtesy of Libby Gardner.)

The Jefferson City recreation program was funded by work-study funds to help Appalachian youth with college expenses. Paul Brewer was the volunteer director, and E. Alan Stair, Jim Deaton, and Madge Susong were student assistants. Programs were held at Nelson Merry School and the city recreation area beneath the library. Carson-Newman was also very cooperative, allowing the program to use its track. Before this program, Roy Harmon, Paul Brewer, and other interested adults began a Little League program in the area. Several teams competed every spring and early summer. Older boys competed in a Babe Ruth League, playing their games at Magnavox Field. Little League baseball is still played on the field at Roy Harmon Park. (Courtesy of Paul and Imogene Brewer.)

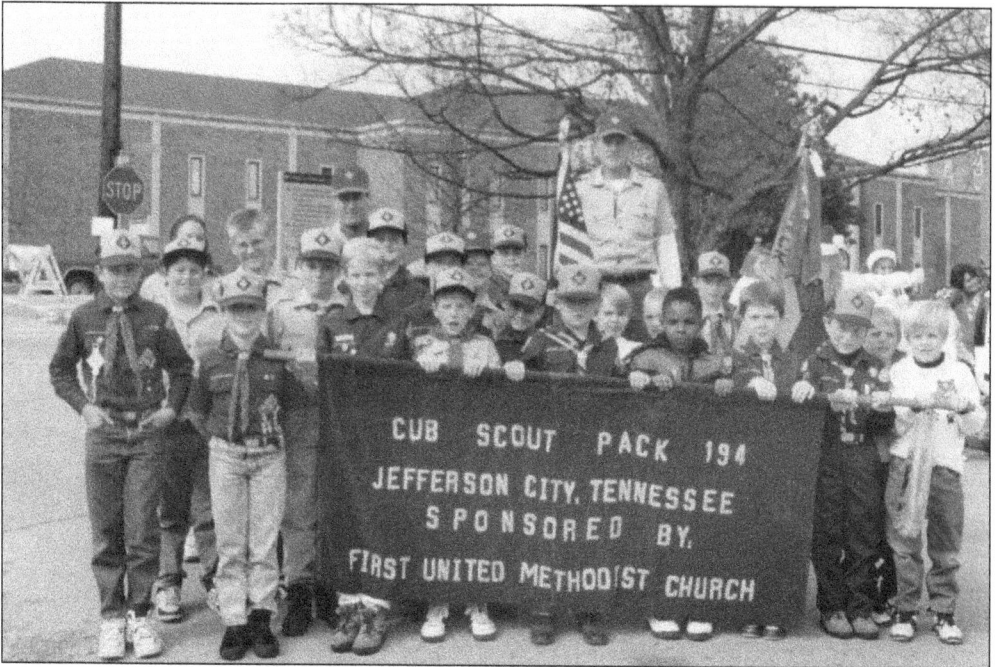

These Cub Scouts had their banner ready to march in the annual Christmas parade and paused for a photograph in front of Carson-Newman's Music Building. Wiley Day was the cub master. (Courtesy of Ronnie Housely.)

Retired teacher Frank Brown is a familiar site with his big-wheel bicycle in each and every Fourth of July, Christmas, and Carson-Newman homecoming parade. His colorful outfits and the decorations on his bike match on each occasion.

The community center was built in 1996 and houses an indoor pool, a walking track, a weight room, and exercise and meeting rooms. It also provides activities for young and old alike, including water aerobics, gymnastics, swim lessons, and basketball.

Jefferson City is within an hour's drive of the Great Smoky Mountains National Park, America's most visited national park. The park provides opportunities for hiking, camping, picnicking, quiet drives, and beautiful scenery, especially in the spring and fall.

Visit us at
arcadiapublishing.com